LIGHTING THE WAY

A History of the Copper Harbor Lighthouse

Barry C. James

Fort Wilkins Natural History Association
Copper Harbor, Michigan
2000

Text Copyright © 1999 by Barry C. James

Publisher:
    The Fort Wilkins Natural History Association
    Fort Wilkins State Park
    P.O. Box 71
    Copper Harbor, Michigan 49918

Book Designer:
    Susan E. Cooper Finney, Howell, Michigan
    Designed in Quark Xpress Version 4.0 on a Gateway G6-400 computer
    Typeface: Garamond Book

Cover Illustration Copyright © 1998 by Susan E. Cooper Finney
    All rights reserved.

Printer:
    Greenlee Printing Company
    423 Pine Street
    Calumet, Michigan 49913

All Rights Reserved:
    No part of this book my be reproduced or utilized in any form or by any means, electronic or mechanical, including photocopying, recording or by any information storage and retrieval system, without permission in writing from the Author and Publisher.

International Standard Book Number: 0-9675103-0-9

In Memory of My Grandparents Anne and Jerome

ACKNOWLEDGMENTS

Throughout my lighthouse research I have been fortunate to come across many helpful persons at national, state and local institutions, and the author would like to thank the following people for their help in gathering data for this book. For advice and research assistance during my two weeks at the National Archives in Washington, D.C., I am indebted to Angie Vandereedt, Civil Reference Archivist, Dr. Robert Browning, United States Coast Guard Historian, and Dave Snyder, Park Historian at the Apostle Islands National Lakeshore. They all shared important leads and historical resources.

The Department of State, Michigan Historical Center provided encouragement and direction while I conducted research at Fort Wilkins State Park, the State Archives of Michigan, and the National Archives. Thanks go to Upper Peninsula Regional Historian Tom Friggens and State Archivist Leroy Barnett (now retired) for their coordinated efforts in supplying valuable documents, maps, surveyor's notes, and historic prints relating to Copper Harbor and the lighthouse. Staff from the Center's Museum Section assisted by developing the graphics and layout for this book. Where photos didn't exist (or haven't yet been found) Artist Richard Geer patiently sketched — and re-sketched — images to match the historic record as closely as possible. Graphics Arts Designer Susan Cooper Finney created the book's format and worked with me in selecting photographs and period illustrations. She also let me display her talents on the cover of this book.

Other individuals have been helpful in many ways. The staff at the Marquette County Historical Society's John M. Longyear Research Library and Michigan Technological University's Archives and Copper Country Historical Collections helped me find blueprints and historic photographs of early Keweenaw lighthouses. Longtime Copper Country residents Mr. Ken Bracco, Dr. Stanley Martin and Mrs. Ruth Vincent willingly put up with my persistent phone calls and visits. They all shared their memories of the Copper Harbor lighthouse and let me examine their collections and memorabilia. Adaline Bradley, Kathleen Cooley, and Ruth Burghardt all deserve thanks for providing valuable biographical information on the Corgan family.

I would particularly like to express my gratitude to the faculty and staff of Michigan Tech's Department of Social Sciences. The roots of this project extend back to my days as a graduate student at MTU, and grew out of their program in Industrial History and Archaeology. In fact, this book is a revised version of the report that I wrote as part of my Industrial Archaeology degree. From the beginning, professors Kim Hoagland, Larry Lankton, Pat Martin, Terry Reynolds and Bruce Seely provided comments. They also read all or part of the report and suggested improvements to the manuscript. It should be noted, however, that none of these individuals are responsible for any errors in this book. That responsibility lies solely with the author.

BCJ

Marquette, Michigan
September 1999

TABLE OF CONTENTS

Preface 1

Chapter One
The Lighthouse Service and
Copper Harbor, 1840 to 1846 3

Chapter Two
The Copper Harbor Light 19

Chapter Three
Work and Life at the
Copper Harbor Lighthouse 53

Chapter Four
Epilogue 85

Appendix
Contract for Building the
Copper Harbor Lighthouse 97

Bibliography 101

Endnotes 107

Picture Credits 115

Index 117

VIII   LIGHTING THE WAY

PREFACE

In the 1840s, the commercial development of Michigan's copper and iron districts placed increased demands on the Lake Superior shipping industry. Lighthouses and other aids to navigation were needed to guide ships traveling on Lake Superior and around the Keweenaw Peninsula. In 1847 Congress approved funds to build light-stations on Lake Superior. The first Copper Harbor light, a stone tower built in 1848, was replaced by the present lighthouse in 1866. In 1933, the United States Coast Guard moved the beacon to a steel tower (where it continues to serve as a navigational aid). Today, the lighthouse property is part of Fort Wilkins State Park and is administered by the Department of State, Michigan Historical Center, in cooperation with the Department of Natural Resources.

The history of the Copper Harbor lighthouse can best be understood if a general background of the Lighthouse Service is provided. The first part of Chapter One gives a brief background of the establishment and administration of lighthouses in the United States. This section is followed by an overview of the development of Copper Harbor as the focal point of America's first mining boom. The chapter then relates the government's presence in the region, and discusses early attempts at copper mining as integral facets behind the establishment of navigational aids on the Keweenaw Peninsula.

The second chapter discusses the history of the Copper Harbor light. This section details the origins, specifications, construction techniques, and lighting technology of the original lighthouse. The author compares the documentary and archaeological evidence and examines the demise of the original light, the adoption of a standard plan for harbor lights on the Great Lakes, and the events leading to the construction of the 1866 Copper Harbor lighthouse. The analysis suggests the 1866 lighthouse and others were built according to standard plans based on the type of light installed in the lantern.

Chapter Three describes work and life at the Copper Harbor lighthouse. Lake Superior lighthouses tended to be more solitary than other stations because of their location, the distance between lights and the weather. The author compares the Copper Harbor light with other stations on the Keweenaw Peninsula and details duties, isolation, and lifestyles of keepers. A biographical section on the men who served at the Copper Harbor light is also included.

The final chapter brings the history of the lighthouse up to the present. During the 1920s the government began to sell unused portions of lighthouse reservations. Chapter Four details the events leading to the abandonment, leasing and eventual sale of the lighthouse property to the State of Michigan. It closes with the circumstances leading to the establishment of the property as a maritime museum as part of Fort Wilkins State Park.

CHAPTER 1
THE LIGHTHOUSE SERVICE AND COPPER HARBOR, 1840 TO 1846

> *This is probably the only place on Lake Superior that will ever be of value for its minerals.... The country is fine, the harbor large, always accessible and perfectly secure.*
>
> Charles W. Penny, explorer 1840

In some respects, the modern history of Michigan's Upper Peninsula begins with the commercial mining of copper on the Keweenaw Peninsula in the 1840s. From that point, European settlers, explorers, mineral deposits, and Lake Superior are linked in the region's development, with the lake serving as the key transportation artery. But with lake travel came the need for lighthouses. This chapter establishes some important background relating to the Copper Harbor light; one of the first on the lake. First it examines the institutional structure of United States lighthouses, then it turns to early mining activity on the Keweenaw Peninsula and the reasons why lighthouses first became important on the remote Lake Superior frontier.

The Lighthouse Service

The Lighthouse Service had its origins in colonial Boston with the establishment of the first permanent lighthouse on the Atlantic Coast in 1716. Several other lighthouses were constructed along the Atlantic Coast, and until 1789 each colony and state built, maintained, and operated aids to navigation within its boundaries. On August 7, 1789, the newly formed Congress of the United States passed an act giving the Federal Government administration over the nation's lighthouses. When the lights came under the jurisdiction of the Federal Government they were placed under the Secretary of the Treasury. From 1820 until 1852, Stephen Pleasonton served as the General Superintendent of Lights, and his duties consisted of formulating Congressional orders, administering contracts, and overseeing the Lighthouse Service as a whole. A collector of customs nearest the location of lights served as the local superintendent and supervised the construction and operation of the lights within his district. In the early years of lighthouse administration political affiliation, rather than a person's capabilities as a builder or keeper, determined who secured building contracts and appointment to lightkeeper positions. Pleasonton's administration was rigid and the service languished under his care since he was unwilling to adopt the Fresnel lens.

The Fresnel lens consisted of concentric rings of glass that concentrated the light in one direction. Each ring projected slightly beyond the previous one refracting the light into a horizontal beam, or focal plane. The number of rings varied with the size of the lens. The lighthouse system in the United States remained well behind other countries like France and England because these countries had adopted the Fresnel lens.[1]

In 1838 Congress investigated the overall condition and operation of America's lighthouses and divided the Lighthouse Establishment into districts. They split the Great Lakes region into two districts, with all aids to navigation above the Detroit River to the western end of Lake Superior included in the 11th District. Congress appointed a naval officer for each district with orders to inspect and review operations, and many of their reports criticized the lighting apparatus and condition of the buildings. In 1841 Congress earmarked funds for the installation of two Fresnel lenses at Navesink, New Jersey. Mariners plying the Atlantic shoreline overwhelmingly applauded the installation of the "new" lenses. Back in Washington the Fresnel lens

Located near the tip of Michigan's Keweenaw Peninsula, the Copper Harbor lighthouse was part of the Lighthouse Board's 11th District which included all aids to navigation above Detroit to the western end of Lake Superior.

finally met Pleasonton's approval, but he continued to be a stumbling block and installed just two more lenses over the next ten years.[2]

Mariners and merchants alike continued to make complaints to Congress about the lighthouse system, and they finally took action in March 1851, requesting the Secretary of the Treasury to look into the matter.

An investigative board was created that consisted of two senior naval officers, two army engineers, a "scientific civilian," and a naval officer. The board submitted a detailed report describing the deficiencies in the management, operation, and maintenance of lighthouses, and urged the installation of Fresnel lenses. They also recommended that Congress create a board to manage the entire lighthouse system under the Secretary of the Treasury. On October 9, 1852, Congress enacted a law creating the Lighthouse Board, an organization that administered the lighthouse system for nearly sixty years.[3]

While under the supervision of the Lighthouse Board, the U.S. Lighthouse Establishment became an efficient operation and the number of navigational aids throughout the country increased dramatically. In the 11th district, for example, there were just six lights in 1846, and none on Lake Superior. The discovery of Upper Michigan copper and iron deposits brought lake traffic and created a greater demand for more navigational aids; by 1868 the number of lighthouses in the district had jumped to 69, and by 1876 there were 116. As a result more people were needed to supervise the lights on the lakes, and the board appointed an engineer to work with the inspector in each district.[4] Under the direction of the Lighthouse Board, the U.S. Lighthouse Establishment operated one of the best navigational aid systems in the world.

In 1910 the government reorganized the nine member Lighthouse Board and created the Bureau of Lighthouses. The bureau was moved to the Department of Commerce, and from 1910 until 1935 George Putnam served as lighthouse commissioner. Four years after Putnam retired President Franklin D. Roosevelt dissolved the bureau, abolishing the Lighthouse Service and transferring the bureau's personnel to the United States Coast Guard. Today, lighthouses continue to function within the Coast Guard, Department of Transportation, as part of the federal navigation system.

Copper Harbor, depicted here in a view published in 1849, hosted the earliest explorers, missionaries, voyageurs and miners.

Copper Harbor, 1840 to 1846

During its early history Copper Harbor was recognized as one of the best harbors on the south shore of Lake Superior. Oblong in shape, the harbor is nearly three miles long and a mile wide. Explorers, missionaries and voyageurs passing along the rugged coast of the Keweenaw found few harbors of refuge, but Copper Harbor offered shelter and a safe place to land their boats.

Since the arrival of European explorers on Lake Superior, virtually everyone who passed along the coast of the Keweenaw Peninsula knew of the presence of copper along its shores. For centuries Native Americans had traded the red metal across North America. They also shared samples of the mineral with French and British missionaries and explorers. In particular, a vein of copper-bearing rock found outside the eastern cape of Copper Harbor captured the attention of those traveling the lake. Known to voyageurs as *La Roche Verte* (the "Green Rock"); it measured ten feet wide and extended from the shoreline into the depths of Lake Superior. This landmark (remnants of which can still be seen today) contained a variety of minerals, including the green copper silicate chrysocolla that gave the formation its color.

In 1840, Michigan's first state geologist Douglass Houghton, and his assistants Charles Penny and Bela Hubbard, surveyed the Keweenaw Peninsula. Houghton had visited the region before as part of a federally sponsored survey with Henry Rowe Schoolcraft's expedition in 1832, and was familiar with the region's copper deposits. On this trip, however, he returned to record Upper Michigan's mineral deposits. After passing the iron district near Marquette the expedition arrived at Copper Harbor on July 3, 1840, and while there they blasted samples of the famed "green rock," which in Houghton's opinion "could be mined advantageously."[5]

The following year Houghton published his findings in a report to the Michigan Legislature describing the presence of native copper in the Keweenaw Peninsula. In 1841 portions of the report appeared in eastern newspapers stimulating the first mineral "rush" in the country. Businessmen seeking to meet the demands of America's brass and bronze industry focused their attention on Keweenaw copper, and prospectors and explorers alike headed north to stake land claims. Copper Harbor became the central gathering place of mining activity on Lake Superior. Houghton's assistant Penny noted "it [Copper Harbor] is probably the only place on Lake Superior that will ever be of value for its minerals. . . . the country is fine, the harbor large, and perfectly secure."[6] Initially, the harbor served as a supply depot and point of departure for explorers. By the summer of 1843, nearly a thousand copper seekers had set up camp and the harbor was "enlivened with sloops, small vessels, and canoes."[7]

Before mining could begin in earnest the U.S. government had to obtain title to the land. Native American land claims served as the main barrier to white settlement in the region. To remove this barrier, and encourage the exploitation of minerals in the Upper Peninsula, in 1843 the United States signed the Treaty of LaPoint with the Chippewa Indians. The treaty provided the U.S. the western half of the Upper

Douglass Houghton, Michigan's first state geologist, surveyed Copper Harbor in 1832 and 1840. On his second trip he blasted samples of the "green rock" and noted the presence of copper ore. Houghton published his findings which helped trigger the country's first mineral rush in 1843.

Peninsula along with portions of northern Wisconsin and northeastern Minnesota.

After the Treaty of LaPoint was signed, the U.S. War Department established a Mineral Land Agency on Porter's Island (at the entrance to Copper Harbor) to regulate exploration and land claims. General Walter Cunningham, former supervisor of the lead mines in Illinois and Wisconsin, directed the agency. Charged with guarding government interests in the region, the agency leased (and later sold) mineral lands, settled land disputes, and prevented squatters from occupying mineral lands without a permit. In case of civil unrest the government authorized Cunningham to draw upon military support at Fort Brady, some 250 miles distant at Sault Ste. Marie.[8]

When explorers and copper seekers arrived on the Keweenaw it seemed that local law enforcement would not be necessary. Not until a small band of Chippewa Indians refused to surrender their claims on Isle Royale did the government decide to establish a military post on the Keweenaw. In their memorial address to the Secretary of War dated March 15, 1844, Michigan politicians urged a military presence in the copper district. The garrison was needed, they argued, to help with law and order, Indian removal, and possible conflict between miners and Indians.[9]

The War Department quickly responded to their request. After looking at a number of places, including the Montreal River, Ontonagon, and L'Anse, Michigan, the Army choose Copper Harbor as the site for the post because of its safe harbor and proximity to the copper mines. In May of 1844, Companies A & B, Fifth Regiment of Infantry, under the direction of Captain Robert Clary, were transferred from Detroit Barracks with orders to construct a fort. Government officials selected a narrow strip of land between the harbor and Lake Fanny Hooe as the fort's location. A typical mid-19th Century Army post, the fort

Copper Harbor became a supply depot and point of departure for copper seekers. In 1843 the U.S. government built a mineral land agency on nearby Porter's Island to regulate mining activity. In 1844 federal troops built Fort Wilkins (shown here in 1892) to maintain order in the region.

consisted of officers' quarters, mess halls with attached kitchens, company barracks, married enlisted men's quarters, storehouses, and a post hospital. Other support buildings included garrison workshops, stables, a slaughterhouse and a post bakery. Named after the Secretary of War William Wilkins, soldiers completed building Fort Wilkins by the end of 1845.[10]

By the time the troops arrived, the shores of Keweenaw Point were whitened with the tents of "speculators and so-called geologists," and a frontier settlement had formed along the shores of Copper Harbor.[11] Rough mining camps had been established near harbors and shipping points, and mining operations had started at various places along Keweenaw Point. One of the first "locations" was the Pittsburgh and Boston Mining Company, located at the eastern point of Copper Harbor. Backed financially by eastern businessmen, Pittsburgh druggist John Hays directed a crew of eight miners to begin work on the "Green Rock." Eventually, two shafts were sunk on "Hays" Point to depths of forty and sixty feet.[12]

Early mining techniques were crude and miners used hand-held drill steels, sledge hammers, shovels and black powder to drill and blast their way through rock. They cut the copper into small pieces, placed it into "kibbles" or tubs, and raised it to the surface by a hand-or-horse powered whim. Once the copper ore was on the surface it was barreled and moved to the nearest shipping point. From there mine workers loaded the copper onto boats and shipped it to smelters on the lower lakes.

While the Pittsburgh and Boston Company worked the shafts on the eastern point of Copper Harbor, soldiers accidentally discovered a vein of black oxide near Fort Wilkins that produced from 60 to 70 percent pure copper.[13] The company soon abandoned their works on the point and moved its operations across the harbor. There, they expanded their mine workings to include "thirty men, seven or eight log buildings, a store house, and a blacksmith shop."[14] In September 1845, while surveying Township 59 North, Range 28 West, Section 33, William Ives recorded, "There is a Miner's Shaft ... where they are at work in a vein of Copper Ore. There are 2 or 3 houses and a barn ... and a wagon road which runs east of the Fort." The company sank two mine shafts near Fort Wilkins 100 feet apart, and the main shaft reached a depth of about 120 feet. After one year miners eventually raised 70,000 pounds of ore before the company left to begin work at the famous Cliff Mine, 25 miles south of Copper Harbor. The Cliff would later become the first U.S. copper mine to pay dividends to its stockholders.[15]

Despite initial optimism, early companies quickly learned that mining Keweenaw copper was expensive, difficult and dangerous. Faced with limited capital, supply problems and a frontier wilderness, many companies soon quit mining. The Pittsburgh and Boston's mines at Copper Harbor followed this same pattern. The cost of bringing in equipment, hiring workers, and building mine facilities and living quarters added up. After nearly two years of mining the shafts on Hays Point and near Fort Wilkins the company made about $3000, despite an investment of about $25,000.[16] Even so, this early mining venture was significant as one of the first commercial efforts to mine Lake Superior copper. Perhaps more importantly, it confirmed the presence of a rich body of ore and fueled the rush for Keweenaw copper.

The establishment of the Keweenaw copper district and nearby settlements created a significant demand for Lake Superior shipping. When explorers and miners arrived on the Keweenaw Peninsula they found an untamed wilderness, and travel overland was limited to a few miles at best. Rugged hills, thick forests, meandering rivers and swamps slowed progress. Roads, if they existed at all, were often little more than twin ruts created by wagons, loaded with in-coming supplies or out-going copper. As one pioneer recalled:

> Not a road or trail existed anywhere on the [Keweenaw] point, and the tangled growth of spruce and white cedar obstructed the banks of the streams and the coast, giving a most unpromising appearance to the country. The only houses that had been erected were the office of the Mineral Land Agency at Copper Harbor, and a crude log hut at Eagle Harbor for the accommodation of explorers.[17]

Transportation by water, although blocked by winter ice five months of the year, was the only practical means of moving people, equipment and supplies throughout the region. John Abert, Colonel of the Corps of Topographical Engineers, wrote:

> [T]he present mode of exploration, as practiced in that country [Keweenaw Peninsula], is both unsatisfactory and expensive, three-fourths of travel being by water in small boats and canoes.... it is considered a good day's work to cross Keweenaw point from Copper Harbor to the mouth of the Montreal river — distance only six miles; whereas eighteen miles round by water is only a half day's journey.[18]

The impassibility of the rapids at Sault Ste. Marie added to travel difficulties. Before the construction of a lock, supplies and small vessels were carried around the rapids to reach Lake Superior. In 1853 Michigan hired the St. Mary's Falls Ship Canal Company to build a lock. The project was directed by engineer Charles T. Harvey, and despite many difficulties, including labor strikes, epidemics, and poor weather, the canal was finished two years later.

In 1844, only two supply vessels operated on Lake Superior. The schooner *Algonquin* and the American Fur Company's brigantine *John Jacob Astor* transported men, equipment, and supplies to mining and fishing ports on the frontier. However, the wreck of the *Astor* proved that the supply line could be easily broken. While carrying supplies destined for Fort Wilkins, a gale pushed the vessel ashore at Copper Harbor on September 21, 1844. Captain Benjamin Stannard described the wreck:

> The brig broke her heaviest anchor and drifted so near the shore that it was impossible for us to get her underway to clear the rocks, our only chance was to ride it out hoping our anchor and chain would hold. . . . In this condition we remained . . . until She dragged ashore on the rocks near the landing at the Fort.[19]

The loss of the *Astor* shocked the western settlements at a moment when they were stockpiling supplies for winter. Mining companies, businessmen, and ship owners demanded a larger shipping fleet, yet in 1845 just three small schooners served the entire Lake Superior region. By 1846, however, one paddle steamboat, one propeller-driven steamer, and ten schooners were plying the lake.[20]

The mariners and explorers who traveled around the Keweenaw Peninsula had few routes to choose from. When approaching the Keweenaw by water from the East, mariners could either travel up Portage River and Lake

Prevailing winds, rocky shores and few harbors put ships rounding Keweenaw Point at risk. One of Lake Superior's earliest shipwrecks was the *John Jacob Astor*. It went ashore during a gale at Copper Harbor in September, 1844.

and walk a mile over land to reach the west side of the peninsula, or travel around the point. Since canoes and "bateaux" could usually be carried, the portage provided the best route.[21] Yet explorers in heavier vessels had no choice but to make the long, dangerous detour around the Keweenaw's tip.

The trip around Keweenaw Point was extremely hazardous. The peninsula juts out like a finger 75 miles into the lake, and strong wind and waves could make navigation difficult for vessels of any size. Protected from north, northwest, and west winds Keweenaw Bay provided boats with limited shelter. Still, vessels rounding the point faced the full force of Lake Superior. Mariners could either hug the shoreline and pass between the point and Gull Rock, or travel around Manitou Island to reach the west side of the peninsula. The experience of Lieutenant James Allen, who along with Houghton traveled with

Schoolcraft's 1832 expedition to Lake Itasca, illustrates the dangers of rounding the point without knowing where to seek shelter:

> This is a dangerous part of the coast for boat navigation. The peninsula offers no safe harbor for boats on its extremity, or near it, on the south side, and we were anxious to get into harbor on the north side before dark. . . . darkness, a strong head wind, and a thick fog soon overtook me as I turned the eastern point. I was then obliged to grope my way for several miles along a high rocky shore, of most forbidding aspect, against which I was in continual danger of being dashed to pieces.[22]

Lake Superior's deadly combination of wind, waves and fog, and the Keweenaw's rock-bound coast, made Copper Harbor a valuable refuge for lake travelers. Since much of Lake Superior (including the Keweenaw Peninsula) was uncharted, and the government had yet to built permanent lighthouses, early navigational aids were maintained at private expense. When entering Copper Harbor, vessels passed between Porter's Island and Hays Point, dodging submerged reefs that make the entrance challenging. At first, mariners built fires or sent out lamps to guide vessels into the harbor. But these offered little help, for as the Reverend John H. Pitezel noted, "We had once before entered this [Copper] harbor in the night . . . when our only beacon was a globe lamp, sent out in a yawl, and placed upon the lone rock in the channel."[23]

By the mid-1840s government officials began to recognize the importance of Copper Harbor to lake shipping and the need for a permanent light. George N. Saunders, Assistant Supervisor of the Mining District, reported to the Secretary of War that "the superiority of the harbor is such, that any other improvement other than a lighthouse would be superfluous; this, however, is important."[24]

Many early visitors to the Copper Country published accounts that depicted Lake Superior's rugged and scenic shore.

John R. St. John, who visited the region in 1845, cited the need for a lighthouse, "or at least a beacon," at Copper Harbor. He also suggested that lighthouses be established at Keweenaw Point, Whitefish Point, and at La Point, Wisconsin.[25] As public pressure mounted, local officials and politicians continued to complain about the need for navigational aids on the frontier. In his report to the Superintendent of Mines Andrew Gray wrote:

> The rapid progress and comparatively immense immigration to Lake Superior, calls for the immediate attention of the government . . . of facilitating and protecting the lives and the property of the people.... Lighthouses should be erected to guide the numerous vessels that are now floating there, and other improvements for their safety are required.[26]

In 1846, delegates from throughout the United States gathered in Chicago, Illinois, to debate the necessity of improving harbors and rivers in the frontier. They also discussed the constitutionality of allocating funds for improving salt water coasts versus similar works on fresh waters. The debate focused on two issues: the remoteness of recently settled areas, and the practicality of spending money toward improving navigational aids on the frontier of the United States. In the end, they agreed that improvements to navigation on the frontier, including Lake Superior, were necessary. In one writer's opinion the convention served as the harbinger of most of the lighthouses, buoys, breakwaters and piers on the upper Great Lakes.[27]

CHAPTER 2
THE COPPER HARBOR LIGHT

Copper Harbor Light is an important Light to general navigation. It was erected in 1848 — and is considered a good light.... No repairs except whitewashing has been done since its erection — and this was done last year

Charles Avery, Superintendent of Lights,
District of Michilimackinac, 1851

During the early years of lighthouse construction a good portion of the material needed to build these structures came from the site where the lights were built. The government did not build light-stations according to standard designs, but in later years the United States Lighthouse Board adopted general plans for lighthouses. This chapter begins with an examination of the origins, specifications, construction, and function of the first Copper Harbor lighthouse, and compares the written record with archaeological evidence. It then describes the original lighting apparatus and the installation of the Fresnel lens. Finally, the chapter turns to the circumstances surrounding the demise of the original light and ends with the events leading to the construction the new Copper Harbor light in 1866.

Congressional approval

On March 3, 1847, Congress approved funds to build several lighthouses, including the Copper Harbor and Whitefish Point lights on Lake Superior. The federal government needed to obtain title to the land for the lights before construction could begin, so the Michigan legislature ceded jurisdiction of certain tracts of land for the "construction and maintenance of lighthouses."[1] The state passed an act that set aside ten acre sites at Monroe, Clinton River, Point Aux Barques, Saginaw Bay, Detour, Whitefish Point, and Copper Harbor. Following the land transfer, Congress appropriated $5000 each to build the first lighthouses on Lake Superior at Copper Harbor and Whitefish Point on April 3, 1847.[2] Two months later the General Land Office reported that Township 59 North, Range 28 West and Sections 2, 3, and 4 in Township 58 North, Range 28 West was selected as the site for a lighthouse at "Copper Harbor, Fort Wilkins, Lake Superior."[3]

Between 1820 and 1852 the supervision and construction of lighthouses rested with the United States Treasury Department. Throughout this period Stephen Pleasonton served as the Superintendent of Lights for the Lighthouse Establishment. His duties included administration of contracts, appointment of keepers, and designation of local collectors of customs to serve as lighthouse superintendents within their districts. Lighthouses on Lake Superior were part of the Eleventh District, which included all navigational aids north of Detroit. The management of Lake Superior lights belonged to the collector of customs at Michilimackinac, in the straits between Lake Michigan and Lake Huron. In 1846, the District of Michilimackinac had just five lighthouses at Thunder Bay, Bois Blanc, Presque Isle, South Manitou, and Pottowatomie.[4] Two years later it would include the Copper Harbor and Whitefish Point lighthouses.

Before construction at Copper Harbor could begin, the government needed to select a building site and advertise for lighthouse bids. Pleasonton ordered the collector of customs from Detroit, Charles G. Hammond, to pick sites at Copper Harbor, Whitefish Point and Point Detour. Pleasonton probably chose Hammond, rather than the

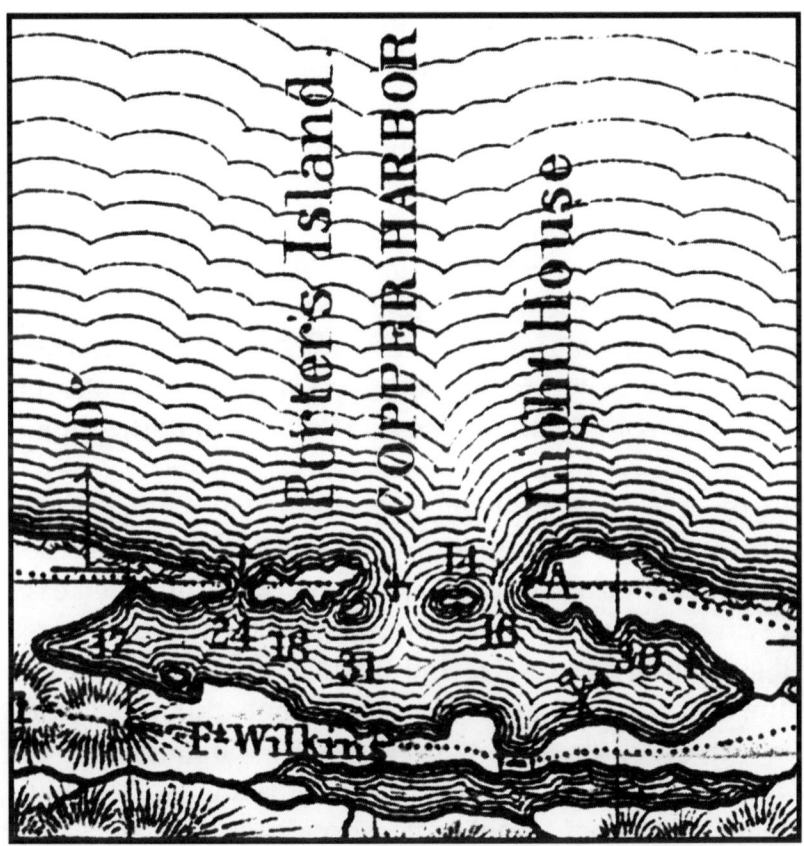

Early travel on Lake Superior was difficult because no permanent lights marked the shoreline. Recognizing the importance of Copper Harbor as a port of call, the U.S. Lighthouse Establishment built a light-station in 1848. It was operational the following year.

superintendent at Michilimackinac, because Detroit served as the headquarters for lighthouses within the district. A newspaper article dated June 12, 1847, reported that Hammond had "recently visited" Copper Harbor to select the lighthouse site.[5] A map published in 1850, entitled *Geological Map of Keweenaw Point, Lake Superior, Michigan*, showed that Hammond chose the eastern point of the harbor for the lighthouse site.[6] It is likely that he picked this location because it marked the eastern end of Copper Harbor and provided building materials like stone, gravel and sand for construction.

After Hammond selected the lighthouse site, Samuel K. Haring, district Superintendent of Lights at Michilimackinac, advertised the construction specifications in newspapers throughout the region. Haring sent proposals to several newspapers, including the *Detroit Democratic Free Press*, *The Chicago Democrat*, *The Lake Superior Miner*, and *The Lake Superior Miner's Journal*. The advertisements ran in these papers from July 6 through August 14. By early August Pleasonton had yet to hear from Haring, causing concern that the money set aside to build the lights to specifications were too low and the lights would not be built during the year. On August 18, 1847, Pleasonton wrote, "I am apprehensive that you will receive no offers to build towers of 65 feet for sums not exceeding the appropriation of $5,000 each, in which case it will be necessary to advertise again for towers 30 feet high with the usual size and build of a keeper's house."7 However, Haring quickly received nine proposals, with bids ranging from a low of $3,863 to a high of $6,300. On August 21, 1847, Charles Rude, of Sandusky City, Ohio, signed a contract to build the Copper Harbor light tower and dwelling for $4,800 (Appendix).8

With the building (and shipping) season limited to May through October, Pleasonton put off the construction of the Copper Harbor and Whitefish Point lights until the next year. The delay provided time for locals to voice their opinions regarding the location of Keweenaw lights. When navigation opened in May of 1848, a group of petitioners requested that the Copper Harbor lighthouse site be changed to Manitou Island (located off the tip of the Keweenaw Peninsula). The site should be changed, they argued, because the light couldn't be seen until a ship had gone three or four miles past Keweenaw Point. A concerned Samuel Haring wrote to Washington stating "there is great opposition to the site selected for the lighthouse at Copper Harbor."9 His supervisor, Secretary of Treasury Robert J. Walker, acted swiftly and on July 8 Congress passed

Joint Resolution 33, authorizing to change the site to Manitou under the stipulation that the work be done at the same price as Copper Harbor. The contractor made preparations to move the construction crew, but the cost of material and labor ran too high. In the end, the Secretary of the Treasury ordered Rude to build the Copper Harbor light-station "as originally agreed upon."[10] The light on Manitou Island would have to wait until the one at Copper Harbor was finished.

In the 1840s and 1850s the government did not have a schematic plan for constructing lighthouses. Instead, there were four sizes of towers, but each structure reflected the characteristics of the surrounding terrain and the availability of local materials. The main variables in lighthouse design were the height of the tower, the intensity of the light, and the location of the dwelling in reference to the tower. The height depended on how far above the water the tower's base was situated and how far the light needed to be seen. At Copper Harbor, it was also important that the light mark the entrance to the harbor. The intensity of the light depended upon the number and size of the reflectors, which determined the size of the lantern on top of the tower. And the location of the light tower and dwelling in connection to one another was adjusted to fit the conditions. Normally, a tower and dwelling came in three forms: a tower attached to the dwelling, a tower attached to the dwelling by a covered walkway, or a tower with a detached dwelling. At Copper Harbor, the light-station followed this last pattern, with a separate keeper's house some 131 feet (40 meters) south and east of the tower. The engineer probably chose to separate the tower and dwelling because the eastern point of Copper Harbor consists of alternating ridges of conglomerate rock eight to ten feet high, thus making construction difficult. In addition, the location of the dwelling provided a level building surface, shelter from prevailing wind and waves, and a convenient spot for landing supplies.

Work commenced sometime after August 21, 1848. Contractor Charles Rude should have started building the light-station earlier, but it took too long for the government to receive bids on the project. The contract specifications called for:

> The lighthouse to be built of split stone or hard bricks in the form round. The foundation to be sunk three feet, ... to be built up solid, and laid in good lime mortar. The tower to be 65 feet high from the surface of the ground, the diameter of the base ... 25 feet and that of the top 12 feet ... the thickness of the walls at the base to be five feet and uniformly graduated to two feet at the top....

> [T]he outside wall to be pointed with Romany cement, and white washed twice over, [with] six windows in the tower, of twelve lights each of ten by eight glass in strong frames and a door 5 feet by 3 feet... the ground floor ... paved with brick or stone....

> The whole to be completed in a workman like manner by the first day of July next, subject to the approval of the Collector of Michilimackinac.[11]

During the early days of lighthouse building the cost of transporting material to the site was extremely high. In 1849 a contractor who proposed to build the lighthouse on Manitou Island lamented that "work cannot be done as cheaply in that country [Keweenaw Peninsula] as in this [Cleveland], the men and provisions, lumber and iron all must be taken from here and carried some 800 miles."[12] Instead of moving goods over great distances, builders often relied on local materials for the bulk of their structures — materials like sand, wood and stone. At the eastern end of Copper Harbor builders found rock (basalt) for the foundation and wall of the light tower. Indeed, the contractor may have used waste rock from the Pittsburgh

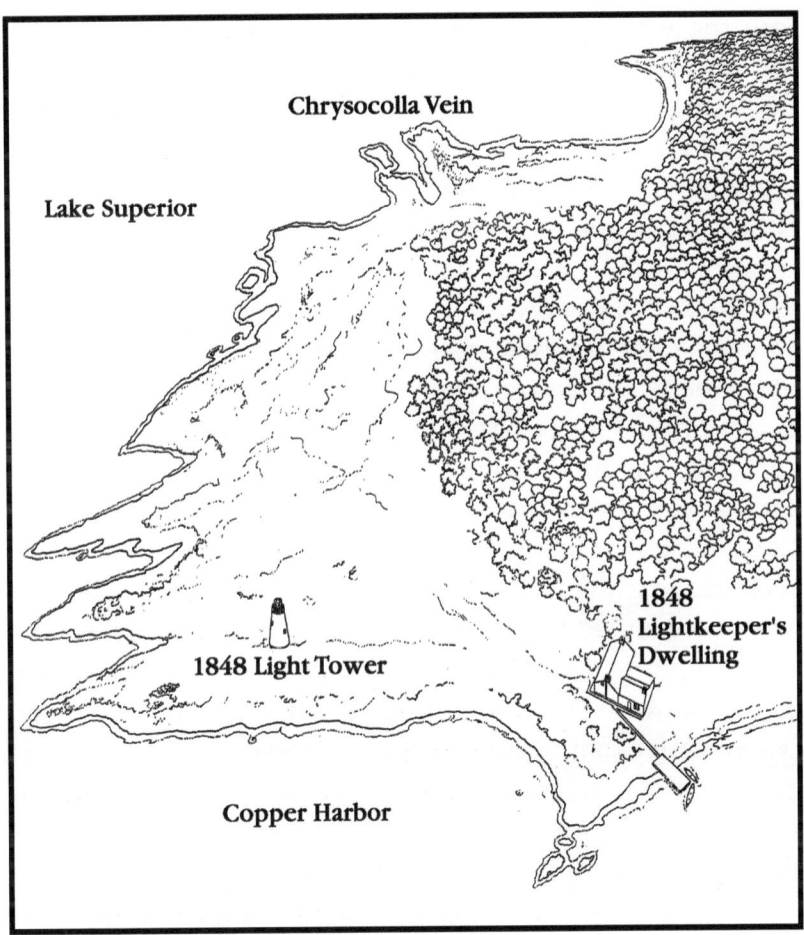

The first Copper Harbor light-station, shown in this artist's rendition, included a stone tower, keeper's house and boat landing.

and Boston mining works nearby.[13] After being quarried the rock was split and shaped by masons and then placed in circular courses. Masons filled the gaps between courses with mortar, probably made from sand, gravel, and calcite found along the shoreline of Copper Harbor and Lake Superior.

During the 1840s and 1850s lighthouse builders commonly used "French plate glass" when finishing a tower's lantern and windows. A few windows were positioned near stairs and landings to provide natural light into the tower. According to Pleasonton's 1851 report to the Lighthouse Board, lantern windows ranged in size from 16 to 28 inches to 5 x 2½ feet, depending on the size of the lantern and type of lighting apparatus. Small panes of glass were held in place by putty, larger panes by pins, and the largest with iron sash bars and screws.[14] The contract for Copper Harbor stated that the top of the light tower be arched, and capped with a deck (14 feet 6 inches diameter) of soap stone "or other stone of proper quality." On one side of the deck was an iron framed and copper plated "scuttle" door (24 x 20 inches) that let the keeper enter the lantern.

Inside the first Copper Harbor light tower a center post carried circular wooden steps leading from the ground to the lantern. The steps consisted of yellow pine "clear of sap and well seasoned." Once the keeper reached the top of the steps an iron ladder provided access to the lantern by way of the "scuttle" door.[15] Many lighthouses built in this fashion had whitewash and plaster on the tower's inside. However, when Michigan Technological University's Industrial Archaeology Program conducted archaeology on the site of the first light tower in 1994, they found no evidence that the Copper Harbor tower was plastered on the inside.[16]

The top of the 1848 Copper Harbor light consisted of an octagonal lantern built of wrought iron angle posts "run down five feet into the stone or brick work." The contract stated that the height and diameter of the lantern be sufficient to:

> ... admit an iron sash in each octagon to contain fifteen lights with fifteen by twenty-four glass ... glazed with an iron framed door covered with copper four feet by two in the clear. ... The top to be a dome framed by sixteen iron rafters concentrating in an iron hoop ... covered with copper.

Attached to the top of the dome were a copper vane and an iron "traversing ventilator" that allowed smoke to escape from the lighting apparatus. As a precaution against

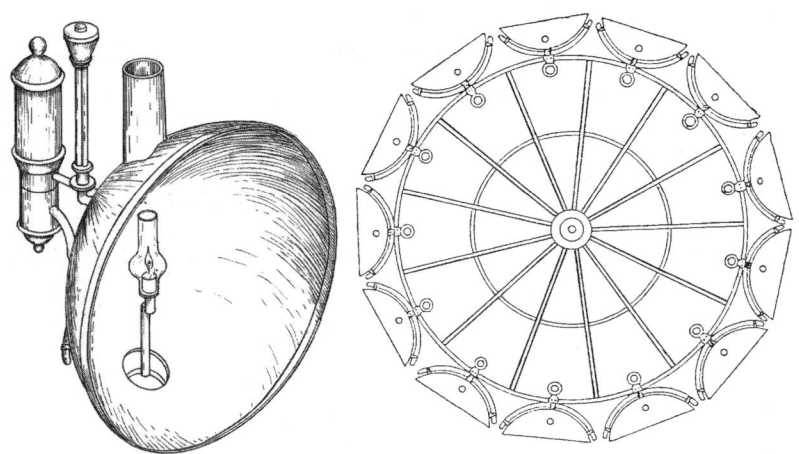

The first Copper Harbor light tower was fitted with 13 Argand lamps with reflectors (left) mounted in a stationary frame called a chandelier (right).

lightning builders attached a copper rod to the ground at the base of the tower, and extended it from the base to about four feet above the ventilator. When finishing the lantern, builders covered the ventilator and dome with copper, painted it black, and painted the interior of the lantern white.[17]

The exterior of a lighthouse also served as a landmark. When approaching from the water a mariner could see several identifiable features such as the number of balconies near the top of the light, the tower's design (whether cylindrical, hexagonal, or octagonal). Also, the keeper sometimes painted the exterior of a light tower to help mariners as a day mark. Colors included red, white, or black, and stripes or bands were used to accent exteriors. Some buildings were left the natural color of the brick or stone.

The original lighting apparatus

Between 1813 and 1851 Winslow Lewis, a former ship captain and friend of Secretary of Treasury Stephen Pleasonton, contracted to provide all lighthouses in the

United States with lamps and reflectors. The lighting apparatus at the first Copper Harbor light-station consisted of thirteen patent lamps and thirteen fourteen-inch reflectors made by Winslow Lewis and Hooper and Company of Boston, Massachusetts. The lamps used in this lighting system were "Argand" lamps. These iron lamps featured a hollow circular wick that produced little smoke.[18] Behind each lamp Lewis placed a "parabolic" reflector, either positioned vertically or dipped toward the horizon to shine the light in the desired direction. The reflectors had a "wash bowl" shape, and each reflector was plated with six ounces of silver to enhance the light.[19] A central stationary "chandelier," equipped with rings and yokes, held the lighting apparatus together. The chandelier also had adjustment screws, catches, and slots to keep the lamps and reflectors steady.[20]

Although no written classification of lights existed from the 1840s to mid-1850s, ship captains could identify each light by the way it operated, whether it flashed or not, and its shape and color. Possibilities included fixed white, revolving white, fixed red, alternating white and red, and double or triple fixed lights. For a fixed (or stationary) light reflectors were arranged around a solid frame or chandelier. Rotating lights were moved by falling weights similar to the mechanisms in a clock. The first light established at Copper Harbor showed a fixed white light that could be seen a distance of about five miles, or six to seven kilometers.[21]

During the 1850s all light-stations on the Keweenaw emitted fixed white lights, but with the expansion of lighthouses in the 1860s the board changed their characteristics to help mariners with identification. The number of Lake Superior lights increased from just two in 1848 to thirteen in 1866. To avoid confusion between lights, the Manitou Island and Eagle Harbor lights were changed to revolving and flashing lights. In 1867 the Lighthouse Service installed the first colored light on the Keweenaw, a fixed red light at Gull Rock, to distinguish it from other lights on the point.[22]

Early lighthouse fuels varied, but United States lights at the time the first Copper Harbor light was built used whale and colza or rapeseed oil. Considered the best and cleanest fuel, whale oil burned evenly and provided a bright light. At Copper Harbor, the keeper used sperm oil. Two "strains" of oil were used: a thick strain known as summer oil and a thinner viscosity for use during winter. To help keepers in maintaining the oil's thickness, the Lighthouse Service equipped many stations with a warming stove to heat the oil so it would burn properly.

In the 1860s the government began to look for a cheaper and more economical fuel to replace whale oil. Due to over hunting, whale oil had become scarce and had increased in cost. For example, in 1841 oil cost just 55 cents per gallon, but by 1848 it had risen to $1.07 per gallon, and by 1855 to $2.25 per gallon. As an alternative the board first turned to colza or rapeseed oil, which had been found to work for the French Lighthouse Service. As a fuel colza oil burned well, produced a better light, and was half the price of whale oil.[23] The U.S. Lighthouse Board attempted to encourage farmers to grow wild cabbage, from which the oil was obtained, but they failed to meet the demand. Thus, the board's committee on experiments, headed by Professor Joseph Henry of the Smithsonian Institution, turned to lard oil and found it burned well if preheated. At Copper Harbor, lard oil served as the main fuel source until the board experimented with kerosene (mineral oil) in the late 1860s. At first the board refused to use kerosene because of the threat of fire. However, by 1876 lard began to give place to kerosene, with the conversion taking place at Copper Harbor in September of 1879 and at Gull Rock in 1880. By 1886 all U.S. lighthouses used kerosene as their primary fuel source.[24]

Description of the original light

Charles Rude and his construction crew arrived at Copper Harbor sometime after August 21, 1848 to build the first Copper Harbor light-station. They arrived late in the year and continued working well into the fall season. It is possible that while at Copper Harbor they lodged at one of the hotels in the village, or after they built the keeper's dwelling they might have stayed there. The construction crew finished building the tower, keeper's dwelling and landing facilities by the end of the 1848 shipping season at a final cost of $4,907. An 1858 inspection report sheds light on how well Charles Rude followed contact specifications for the tower and keeper's house.[25] It is obvious from the inspection that the builders "cut a few corners." The 1858 report lists the color of the tower as white, made of stone, with a height from the base to the lantern deck of 44 feet. The tower walls were four feet thick at the base with an interior diameter of thirteen feet; they were two feet six inches thick at the top with an interior diameter of eight feet six inches. To let light into the tower it had four windows of twelve 8 x 10 panes of glass. The inspector noted that the staircase consisted of wood, and that the watch room served as a storage room for oil in the tower.[26]

According to the 1858 report the tower had an "eight sided" lantern with an interior diameter of ten feet six inches. The lantern consisted of twelve panes of glass on each side measuring 24 x 15 inches; the lantern "cowl" or dome was made of copper and had two ventilators. It emitted a fixed white light 65 feet above lake level, and had two "fountain lamps."

When the inspector examined the 1848 keeper's dwelling he described it as painted white and made of stone with a shingled roof. Inside the house he noted four painted rooms; a sitting room, two chambers, and a kitchen. The exterior dimensions of the dwelling were 34 x 20 feet, with an attached kitchen measuring 15 x 24 feet. "One wood stove" provided both heat and cooking facilities. He also noted that the building and grounds lacked a cistern and well, suggesting that the lake served as the water supply.[27]

Some data from the 1858 description (above), archaeological investigations, and Rude's contract doesn't make sense. The most obvious contradictions relate to the dimensions and height of the stone tower. Michigan Tech's archaeological investigations during the summer of 1994 discovered remains of the tower's foundation in *situ*. Beneath a topsoil layer and extensive basalt rubble from the demolition of the structure, short segments of the bottom course of stone were found still mortared together and attached to the conglomerate bedrock. It is clear from these excavations that Charles Rude did not build the tower to specifications because the contract called for the walls of the tower to be five feet thick at the base with a total diameter of 25 feet. However, when excavated the stone foundation measured about 22 feet (6.8 meters) diameter. This archaeological

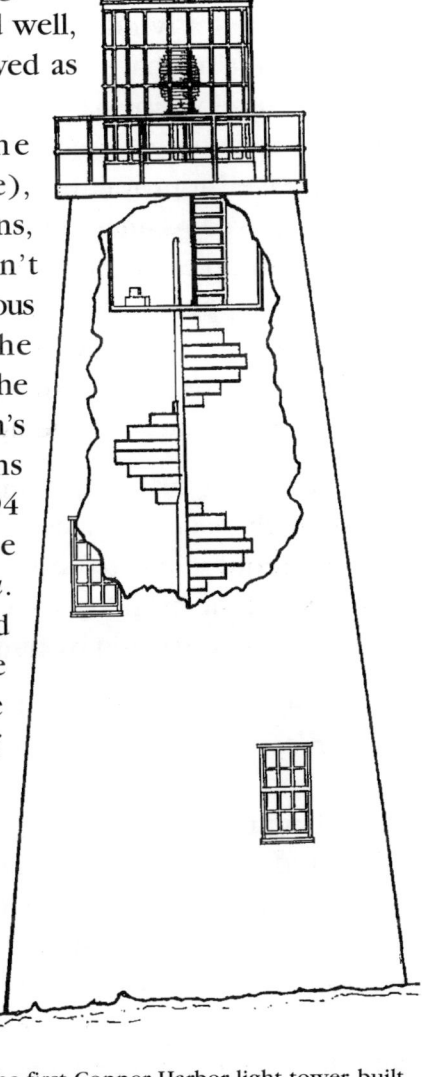

The first Copper Harbor light tower, built in 1848, was 44 feet high and topped with a metal lantern that housed the light.

evidence nearly matched the 1858 report's measurement of the base of the tower as 23 feet.[28] Additionally, the 1858 report lists the tower as 44 feet high with four windows, not 65 feet with six windows as in the contract. Perhaps the contractor did not have enough building material, or enough time at the close of navigation, to build the tower and dwelling to contract specifications. Yet in the end, Rude's work received approval from the local collector of customs, and he received payment upon completion of the contract.

Once completed, the government asked the contractor to stay at Copper Harbor until the arrival of a permanent keeper. In a letter to Pleasonton dated January 15, 1850, Charles Rude described the circumstances in which he was placed in charge of the lighthouse;

> When the work was completed and I was about taking the men away, the Colector [sic] of makcanaw [sic] request me to leave one man there to take charge of the property which was subject to be taken away and destructed by hunters and trappers.[29]

Rude assigned his building partner, Ebenezer Warner (the builder of the Whitefish Point lighthouse), to stay the winter and secure the property until the keeper arrived. On February 24, 1849, the Secretary of the Treasury appointed Henry Clow, a former soldier at Fort Wilkins, as the first keeper of the Copper Harbor light. The government provided him with an instruction list and requested that he live in the dwelling at all times. Clow worked as keeper at Copper Harbor from February 1849 until his resignation in August 1853, and received $350 per year for his services.[30]

It is likely that the Copper Harbor and Whitefish Point light-stations were first illuminated when navigation opened in 1849. Both sites probably had temporary beacons, but as a rule Lake Superior shipping opened in mid-April and closed in late November or early December.

Pleasonton hired a keeper at Whitefish Point in October of 1848, but the light was not fully operational until the following year. In 1849, Charles Avery, Superintendent of Lights in the Michilimackinac District, submitted his first quarter report in January, but neither the Copper Harbor nor Whitefish Point lights were listed because the shipping season had yet to open. On June 5, 1849, however, Avery's second quarter report requested $87.50 each to open the lights at Copper Harbor and Whitefish Point.[31] Thus, the Copper Harbor and Whitefish Point lights share the distinction of being the first government built lighthouses operating on Lake Superior.

The government built two more lighthouses on Lake Superior, at Manitou Island (1849) and Eagle Harbor (1850). The erection of three lights on the Keweenaw Peninsula shows the relative importance of lights in the copper region (there were just five U.S. lights on Lake Superior at the time). During this period the ports of Copper Harbor, Eagle Harbor and Ontonagon became important shipping centers on Lake Superior's south shore. Mining companies built docks at these places to land in-coming equipment and supplies, and to load out-going copper ore. The Manitou, Copper Harbor, and Eagle Harbor lights served as a chain of lights to guide boats around Keweenaw Point. In practice, the range of these lights overlapped and a ship captain could keep a light within view until sighting the next one. In 1850, while traveling around Keweenaw Point on the propeller steamer *Independence*, the Reverend John H. Pitezel recalled:

> The light-house from Manito [sic] Island shed a soft, clear light, which we saw for miles, till it seemed to sink in the lake. Meanwhile light from the Copper Harbor light-house was now clearly seen.... By the erection of these light-houses a great blessing has been conferred on mariners and the traveling public generally.[32]

The original Copper Harbor light fared better than other lights built on Lake Superior during the late 1840s and 1850s. Most of the lighthouses were similar in design, with stone towers. The Whitefish Point light, situated on the sandy shoreline of Whitefish Bay, needed fixing just one year after its completion. Supposedly built to the same specifications as the Copper Harbor light, its foundation consisted of flat logs laid in the sand. The tower was finished with alternating layers (about 10 feet apart) of stone with timber bracing. One observer described it as "one of the worst built lights on the lakes." The keeper complained that the tower leaked continuously, and that it was nearly impossible for him to keep the light burning. The Marquette lighthouse, built in 1853, wasn't much better. In a report to district headquarters the keeper there noted that the foundation leaked, and during strong winds the tower shook "making it unsafe to perform his duties."[33] The first Copper Harbor light, however, remained in good condition after its completion. During its first few years of operation the tower required general maintenance, such as painting and whitewashing, which were done annually by the keeper or by contract to the lowest bidder. In his 1851 report district supervisor Charles Avery described the lighthouse as follows:

> Copper Harbor Light — is situated at said harbor on Lake Superior and is an important Light to general navigation. It was erected in 1848 — when the lighting apparatus was put up new — It has 13 lamps and is considered a good light. The tower is constructed [of] rough building stone laid in lime mortar and is a tolerable good one — No repairs except whitewashing has been done since its erection — and this was done last year.[34]

In 1853 Henry Clow resigned as Copper Harbor light-keeper. His replacement, Henry C. Shurter, began work on

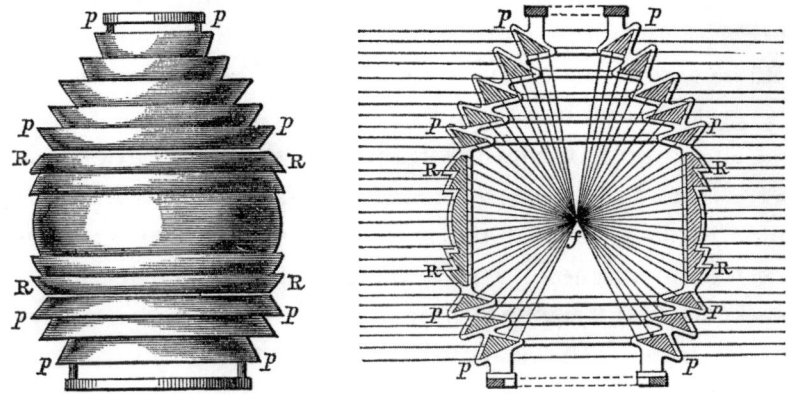

Perfected by French physicist Augustin Fresnel, the Fresnel lens used glass prisms and cylinder refractors to bend the light of a single lamp into an intense beam. Many of these lenses are still used today.

August 5. Shurter's tenure as keeper lasted just a year and a half, for on March 23, 1855, Napoleon Beedon received the appointment as keeper, a position he held for fourteen years.35 While under Beedon's care several changes took place at the lighthouse including the installation of a new lighting device — the Fresnel lens.

Installation of the Fresnel lens

After Congress created the Lighthouse Board it quickly began to upgrade and improve the nation's lighthouses. In 1852, as one of their first actions, they recommended the replacement of Winslow Lewis' lighting apparatus with the Fresnel lens. Far superior to parabolic reflectors, the Fresnel lens was made up of concentric rings of glass that concentrated the light in one direction. Each ring had exquisite glass prisms that refracted the light into a horizontal beam or focal plane. The number of rings varied with the size of the lens. Still used in modern aids to navigation, the lenses are classified into six "orders" based on the focal length of the lens (how far the light can be seen), with one being the largest and six the smallest.

(There are seven sizes because there is a three and a half order lens). Lamps were specially designed for this system and had from one to five wicks. Larger sized lenses required the greatest number of wicks.

The largest of the Fresnel lenses, the First Order lens, were used as seacoast lights. These lights gave warning of the approach to land and are nearly twelve feet high and six feet in diameter. The Second and Third Order lenses marked secondary points or headlands along sea coasts, bays, and sounds, with the Third Order serving as the primary light for the coasts of lakes. Fourth, Fifth, and Sixth Order (or harbor lights) were intended to mark entrances to ports, headlands, shoals in large bays, obstructions in rivers, and piers and wharves. These lights are $19^{5}/_{8}$, $14^{1}/_{2}$, and $11^{3}/_{4}$ inches in diameter respectively.[36]

In 1856 the Copper Harbor lighthouse was fitted with a Sixth Order Fresnel that could be seen for four to six miles in clear weather. For many years French lens builders Barbiere & Fenestre, Henri Le Paute & Suatter, Lemonier & Cie, and the English Chance Brothers supplied the United States with the lenticular apparatus, and by 1859 nearly every U.S. lighthouse was equipped with a Fresnel lens.[37] Costs for the lens varied, but the first Sixth Order lens installed at Copper Harbor ranged from $226.80 for a 270-degree arc, to $219.16 for a 180-degree arc lens. Interestingly, the French government had nearly abandoned using sixth order lights because of their small dimensions and "feeble" illuminating power, but the Lighthouse Board continued to install them in United States lighthouses.[38]

Despite the aid of a new lighting apparatus, shipping accidents still happened at Copper Harbor. Each year vessels attempted to push the shipping season to the limit, and when winter storms and ice threatened lake navigation, supplies were sometimes left at ports some distance from their final destination. During a severe storm in November 1855, the steamers *Superior* and *Ogontz* and schooners

Ford and *Freeman* all took shelter at Copper Harbor. The captains of the *Ogontz* and *Superior* decided to discharge their freight at the dock of Raley and Company and leave for the lower lakes. But the *Ford* and *Freeman* had arrived leaking and covered with ice, so the captains of both vessels decided to "lay up" at Copper Harbor for the winter. Thinking that the shipping season had ended, lightkeeper Beedon closed the light to navigation on November 30.[39]

Upset that some of their winter supplies had not arrived, the residents of Ontonagon hired the schooner *Seaman* to risk the journey north and pick up their supplies. Ironically, the day after keeper Beedon closed the light, the vessel tried to enter Copper Harbor during a gale and landed on the rocks. On December 8, 1855, the *Lake Superior Miner* reported:

The government installed different sizes of lighthouse lenses to mark shorelines, shoals, rivers, islands, harbors and sea coasts. The largest Fresnel lens on the Great Lakes was a second order lens. Most Lake Superior lighthouses had a fourth order lens (shown here in a lantern).

> Capt. Beaser, who went out last week on the Schooner *Seaman* for the purpose of bringing forward our supplies at Copper Harbor, returned overland last evening bringing the disheartening news of the loss of that vessel on the rocks. . . . *There were no Lights in the Lighthouse* . . . but the vessel attempted to beat in, where she now lies a wreck.

In an effort to shift the blame from keeper to boat captain, the keeper's father, John A. Beedon, wrote to his son's supervisor at Michilimackinac trying to explain the incident. John Beedon stated that local residents thought that navigation had closed and that "no one expected or even looked for anything afloat on the lake." The problem, according to Beedon, rested with the vessel since it had broken her main sail and was inoperable.[40]

The people of Ontonagon attempted to get their supplies by "breaking" a road through heavy snow 90 miles to Copper Harbor, but their efforts resulted in limited success. Relief finally came in the spring with the opening of navigation. The first steamer arrived in March and a crew managed to raise the *Seaman* and salvage the vessel.[41] The Lighthouse Board looked into the matter, but the Copper Harbor lightkeeper never faced charges for neglect of duty. Perhaps in hindsight, keeper Beedon reported the light as "too small" the following spring, and recommended a larger lens for the lantern. In fact, he preferred the old system of lighting because the "new" lens didn't work very well. The inspector of the district, George Scott, traveled to Copper Harbor to investigate and confirmed Beedon's report. On May 31, 1857, Scott asked that a Fourth Order lens be installed in the lantern, but the board ignored his request. It would be another two years until the Copper Harbor light finally received a larger lens.[42]

The oversight proved costly. On November 10, 1857, the *City of Superior*, her hull full of winter supplies, attempted to enter Copper Harbor during a gale and grounded on the rocks just in front of the lighthouse. Captain John Spaulding worked desperately to get her off the point and tried to lighten the load by throwing overboard 1500 barrels of flour, but by nightfall he gave the order to abandon ship. "Her going ashore," reported the *Milwaukee Sentinel*, "was caused by a heavy snow storm which hid the light."[43] By morning 15 inches of snow had fallen and the vessel filled with water and broke in two. Its cargo, consisting primarily of flour, beef, pork, corn, and oats, proved a total loss. The Toltec Copper Mining Company took the loss particularly hard as 44 bags of oats, 25 barrels of mess pork, 17 barrels of beef, and 50 barrels of flour never made it to the port of Ontonagon. Because of the shortage of goods the mine had to reduce its workforce until the next spring — it simply couldn't feed all of its employees.[44]

Recommendation for a new lighthouse

In August of 1863, Joshua Barney, a member of the United States Lake Survey and assistant engineer of the 10th and 11th Lighthouse Districts, arrived at Copper Harbor to inspect the lighthouse and keeper's dwelling. It is obvious from his report that the condition of the tower and dwelling had changed drastically since the 1858 inspection. When describing the light tower Barney wrote:

> The walls of the tower are substantially built of rubble masonry. Its base is on a rock foundation and situated in a slight depression between two ridges of rock, which has a gentle declivity towards the tower. The door faces the depression, and the sill being elevated but a [illegible] around the water which accumulates ... to a depth of at least one foot, which can escape only under the walls of the tower.[45]

To correct this problem he recommended that the base of the tower be filled with stone to allow water to escape over the ridges of rock. The tower also had problems with its coping (deck) and lantern (dome). Inspector Barney wrote:

> The diameter of the coping of the tower at fourteen feet, the coping stones are small, making many imprints or seams . . . and the water runs through copiously during rain. . . . The lantern is unusually and unnecessarily large, being ten feet in diameter, and of the old pattern. . . . The keeper informed me that the dome leaked all over.

As a fix he proposed that builders line the tower with brick and iron. He also suggested that a new Fourth Order lantern be installed to replace the old lighting apparatus.

Barney's report also commented on the poor condition of the 1848 keeper's dwelling. He noted that the walls appeared "substantially built," yet the "whole interior" of the structure should be rebuilt. Apparently, while building the house the contractor put the plaster directly against the stone walls and "no studding or nothing whatever" had been used. Without proper insulation the building was difficult to heat. Barney wrote that "air condenses and freezes on the walls" and that keeper Beedon told him "large icicles form whilst good fires are burning in the stoves." He eventually labeled the house as "defective and unsuitable for the climate," and recommended abandoning the keeper's dwelling and building a new one next to the stone tower.[46]

Inspector Barney sent his report to Washington for consideration. By the 1860s the Lighthouse Board had begun to adopt standard plans for lighthouses, and builders no longer relied upon local materials to build aids to navigation. Trained at West Point, officers of the Lighthouse Board received schooling as engineers, and during this period they developed standard plans and modified them to fit their needs.[47] Correspondence from

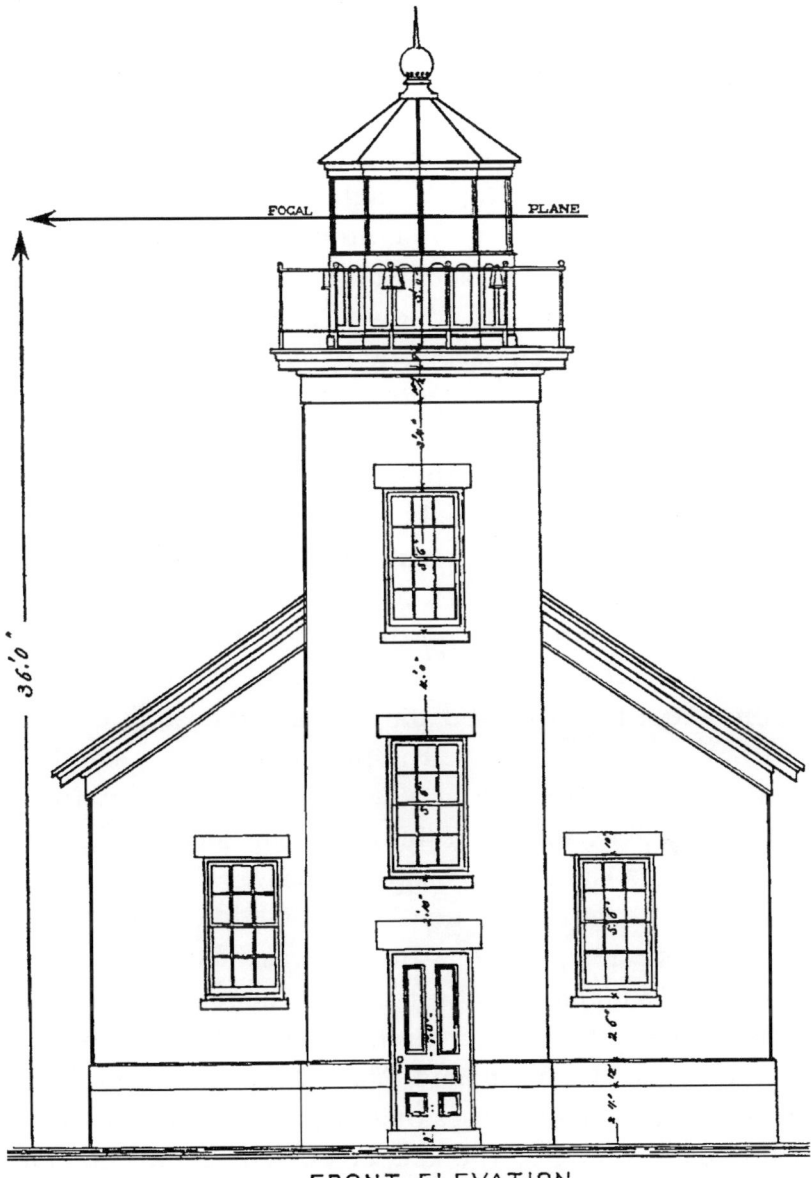

FRONT ELEVATION

In the 1860s lighthouse engineers combined the light and house under one roof by attaching a tower to the dwelling.

the Lighthouse Board confirms this statement, for on November 8, 1863, Colonel Graham, Barney's superior, submitted two plans for rebuilding the Copper Harbor light. The first followed Barney's recommendation of rebuilding the keeper's dwelling and was identical to the plan for renovating the lighthouse at Saginaw Bay, Lake Huron. It called for connecting the tower and dwelling with a covered walkway at a final cost of $10,798.15. The second followed a plan approved for a lighthouse at Green Island, Wisconsin, for $7,494.85.[48] Despite Graham's efforts both plans failed to pass the government's approval.

A year later the Lighthouse Board reported that the original Copper Harbor light "required extensive repairs" and submitted estimates for rebuilding the structure. That summer Colonel William F. Raynolds relieved Graham as Engineer of Lighthouses on the northern lakes. Raynolds, who also served as superintendent of the U.S. Lake Survey, submitted a plan for rebuilding the lighthouse at Copper Harbor on July 23, 1864. His plan exhibited a standard harbor light consisting of a two-story dwelling with an attached square tower on the front, but once again it did not meet the Lighthouse Board's approval.[49]

In 1866, plans for a "new" Copper Harbor light finally cleared the government's bureaucracy when Congress granted $13,600 for its construction. The same design was approved for the Copper Harbor, Marquette, Gull Island, Grand Island, Michigan, and Eagle Bluff, Wisconsin, lighthouses.[50] Most lighthouses built during this period and in later years combined the keeper's dwelling and the light tower under one roof. According to lighthouse regulations the particular order of the lighting apparatus determined the size (and style) of these structures. All of the lights built to this style were fitted with a Fourth Order or smaller lens, and this is the reason many harbor lights (and coast lights) on the Great Lakes are similar in design.

Although the main light on the eastern point led sailors to Copper Harbor's entrance, it could not guide them past dangerous reefs on either side of the channel. In 1865 the federal government built a set of range lights mounted on front and rear towers. In 1868 the Lighthouse Service replaced the rear range light with a keeper's house with an attached tower. Still in service, these lights are located near Fort Wilkins.

The Lighthouse Board built other navigational aids with standard plans as well, including the Copper Harbor range lighthouse. Congress authorized the construction of range lights for entering the harbor as early as 1860, but the lights were maintained at private expense. These lights marked the deepest and safest part of the channel entrance. They are made up of two lights (a front range and a rear range) placed a proper distance apart so the back light is higher than the front one. By lining up the lights one above the other, and using them as a "lead lights," a navigator could safely enter the harbor. In 1865, the War Department transferred the land and buildings at Fort Wilkins to the Lighthouse Board so they could hire a keeper to watch these lights.[51] The keeper lived in one of the fort buildings until the military regarrisoned the fort in 1867, he then moved to the village of Copper Harbor and had to travel over a mile to maintain the lights. Thus, it became necessary for the government to build a keeper's house. In September of 1867 Raynolds wrote to Washington proposing that the government erect a dwelling similar to those under construction at Portage Lake and Grand Island (Munising, Michigan) ranges. Raynolds wanted to remove the rear range light (which was placed on a wooden tower) and place it in the tower of the keeper's house at an estimated cost of $3,951.55, so long as they could transfer the men working on the Portage Lake range lights to Copper Harbor. By transferring the crew to Copper Harbor, they could speed up construction and save money by using resources already in the area. On July 28, 1868, Congress granted an additional $5,000 for the project, and the keeper's house (which is still standing) was completed before the end of the shipping season.[52]

When building lighthouses the government typically contracted for builders to complete more than one light-station during the shipping season. Many different men, with different trades and talents, were needed to build these structures. Workers included carpenters, laborers and masons to build the dwelling, and lampists to install the light in the lantern. A superintendent, usually a lighthouse engineer, accompanied the lighthouse builders to oversee their work and inspect the material and labor. In 1855 the *Lake Superior Journal* reported that the *Fanny and Floy* had passed the Sault Canal with a crew of 50 men and "all

What happened to the first Copper Harbor Light?
For many years some thought it had collapsed into Lake Superior or washed away in a storm. In 1994 archaeologists from Michigan Technological University solved the mystery by excavating the tower site and examing the 1866 lighthouse cellar. They found original painted stone from the 1848 tower had been used as foundation material for the 1866 lighthouse. (Note the whitewashed stones in the photograph).

the necessary materials" for finishing seven lighthouses on Lake Superior. These men were furnished with plans "so full and precise" that the contractor seldom needed further orders to complete the job.[53] Depending on the scope of the work, the size of construction crews varied. While building the Escanaba (Sand Point) lighthouse in 1867, a structure nearly identical to the Copper Harbor light, the government employed twenty-five to thirty men who took six to eight weeks to finish the job.[54] The construction crew at Copper Harbor must have been about the same size.

A lighthouse engineer selected a site 77 feet (24 meters) east of the first Copper Harbor light tower for the 1866 lighthouse. This location placed the new tower on a higher point of land, permitting a shorter tower to have the same focal plane as the original light. But what happened to the 1848 stone tower? Over the years local rumors persisted that the tower had washed away into the lake, probably during a winter or spring storm. One author reported that water had "probably" undermined the tower's foundation. In the end, historical and archaeological evidence provided the answer to this long-standing mystery.[55] In 1994, during Michigan Technological University's investigation of the site, archaeologists examined a semicircular mound with a depression that marked the site of the 1848 tower. Before excavation they recorded and collected samples of split stone (basalt) that were found scattered throughout the site, and some of these samples showed evidence of whitewash on their surfaces. Excavation of the mound uncovered fragments of the foundation still intact, and in some places remnants of cut stone mortared to the conglomerate were found in *situ*. MTU's investigation also revealed fragments of clear and colored glass, square cut nails, remnants of window framing, and cement or mortar. But surprisingly little of the original stone tower remained on-site. In fact, builders had reused the stone as foundation material for the 1866 lighthouse and privy. Careful inspection of the 1866 lighthouse cellar showed that each stone had been reshaped and mortared into place, and many stones showed signs of their original whitewash from use in the 1848 light tower. MTU concluded, based on detailed measurements of the lighthouse and privy foundations, that over 80% of the 1848 tower had been reused to build the base of the 1866 lighthouse.[56]

The new two-story 1866 lighthouse was rectangular in plan, measured 25 1/2 by 29 feet and had 1800 square feet of floor space. Builders attached a 42-foot square tower to the front of the dwelling. The interior diameter of the tower, complete with a 42-step iron circular stairway leading to the lantern, measured six feet six inches. To help mariners a temporary beacon was placed on the point until the completion of the lighthouse, sometime after

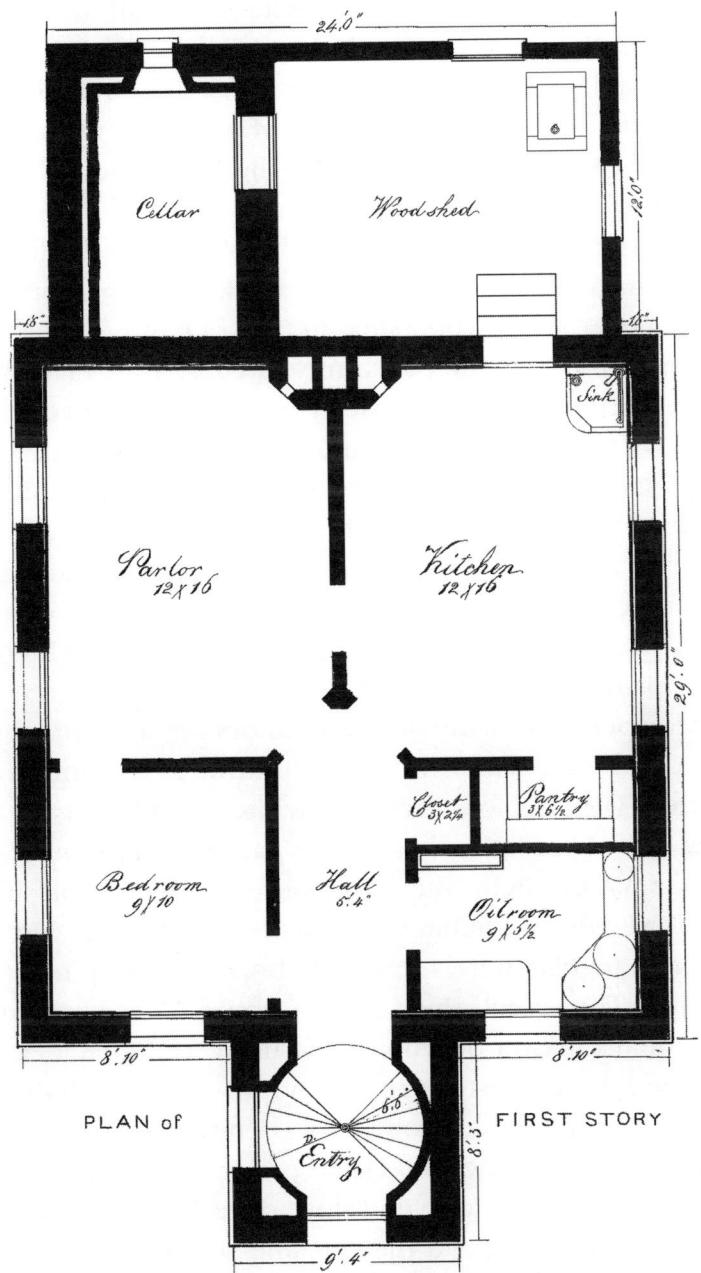

The United States Lighthouse Board used the same design to build lighthouses at Copper Harbor, Grand Island, and Marquette, Michigan. These structures had 1,000 square feet of floor space and included a kitchen sink that could pump water from a cistern.

June 1866.57 The Lighthouse Establishment installed a Fourth Order lens made by H. Lepaulle and fitted it with a set of Franklyn lamps. *Thompson's Coast Pilot*, a publication listing the location and number of aids to navigation on the Great Lakes, characterized the light as fixed white and visible for 10 miles.58

The plan for the Copper Harbor lighthouse called for six rooms on the first floor: a parlor, kitchen, bedroom, oil room, cellar, and a wood shed in the back of the structure. The parlor and kitchen each measured 12 by 16 feet, with the kitchen having an enclosed pantry. Builders covered the walls with lathe and plaster, and all of the rooms except the cellar and hallway were wainscoted to the window sills.

Second floor rooms were painted and accented with different colors (according to regulations). A paint analysis conducted in 1997 determined the lighthouse's original paint scheme, and the ceilings and walls in each room were painted white and the floors a yellow/brown color. The keeper used many different colors for accenting baseboards, doors, window sash, window cases, and wainscoting. These colors included white, off-white, gray, and even a shade of light-pink for the parlor's wainscoting.59

For natural light, the first floor had ten double hung windows with six lights 8 x 10 inches each. Each window had rectangular lintels and sills bordered by pine-green shutters. The second floor of the Copper Harbor lighthouse contained a master bedroom measuring 16 by 18 feet, and included a closet, store room and an unfinished storage space. A chimney, centrally located near the back of the building, provided the wood shed, parlor, kitchen, and master bedroom with flues for wood stoves. The lighthouse exterior had a shingled roof and the east and south sides carried a plank deck equipped with a wooden railing. Builders faced the house, tower and privy with yellow or "Milwaukee Brick." The old 1848 keeper's dwelling remained undisturbed and was used by the keeper as an oil storage area.

From 1883 to 1887 the Copper Harbor light was closed to lake navigation. The lighthouse is shown here around 1900.

Discontinuance of the light, 1883 to 1887

In the 1850s, the discovery of copper near Portage Lake led to the development of the central and southwestern portion of the Keweenaw copper district. Large (and later profitable) mines were being established near the villages of Houghton, Hancock and Red Jacket (Calumet). A few mines were still being worked near Copper Harbor at the Clark, Delaware, Phoenix and Star mines, but the village was becoming less populated and even less important as a shipping center. In 1870 Copper Harbor Township boasted a population of more than 300 people, but a decade later just six families and about 30 people lived in the village. One traveler noted the town had "fallen into decay" and only two students attended the local school.60 Active mines near the tip of the Keweenaw were few and far between, and Copper Harbor changed from a bustling pioneer community into a backwater hamlet.

In 1883 the Lighthouse Board recommended that the Copper Harbor light be closed to navigation. With the completion of the Portage Lake Ship Canal in 1873 (located between Houghton and Hancock), many vessels no longer had to travel around Keweenaw Point. The canal, two miles long, one hundred feet wide and fourteen feet deep, shortened Lake Superior navigation by more than 150 miles. No doubt the construction of the canal impacted the decision to close the Copper Harbor light. The government contemplated raising the rear range light across the harbor to replace the light on the point, but first they needed an investigation. In September the district inspector and engineer arrived to look into the matter. The inspector reported the light on the point wasn't needed because vessels heading east, after rounding Keweenaw Point, could keep both the Manitou and Gull Rock lights in sight until sighting the Copper Harbor range lights. "Vessels approaching from the west," he wrote, generally "kept the Eagle Harbor light in view" until sighting the same range lights.

However, the engineer's report differed from the inspector's. After interviewing captains of the Lake Superior Transit Company and the Ward Line of Steamers the engineer reported:

> [The captains] all seem to regard Copper Harbor as of the utmost importance. . . . during frequent storms in October and November the rounding of

Keeweenaw Point is a dangerous undertaking and the dread of all who navigate Lake Superior. . . . the light itself has always been regarded as one of the very best for brightness and for the nearness with which it could be approached.61

Furthermore, he felt that the rear range could not replace the main light because it was a half mile inside the harbor and could not be seen. "Should . . . the Board deem it advisable to abolish this light," he concluded, "I would recommend that Eagle Harbor light be changed from 5th to 4th order, the same order as Copper Harbor."62

Despite the threat of closing the light, a repair crew still worked on the lighthouse. Repairs included installing lantern glass, mending door steps, and rebuilding the wooden sidewalks around the dwelling. Still, the Lighthouse Board recommended that the light be closed to navigation on October 6. The lightkeeper, James W. Rich, transferred to Gull Rock, and the board placed the buildings and grounds under the charge of the Copper Harbor range lightkeeper. The tender *Amaranth* removed the lens the following year.63

Shipping on the Great Lakes prospered in the 1880s, for water transportation remained the least expensive means of moving goods throughout the region. As shipping increased vessel owners organized associations to promote business. One of the more prominent groups was the Cleveland Vessel Owners Association, created in 1880 to improve common interests such as communication, wrecking privileges, channels, and aids to navigation. The association worked with the Lighthouse Board's Location Committee concerning additions and alterations to beacons, ranges, buoys, and fog signals on the inland lakes in the United States.64 On December 29, 1887, they requested that the Copper Harbor light be relighted, but the chairman of the Lighthouse Board disagreed because he thought the harbor was of "little importance" to lake navigation. Faced with public pressure James W. Watson, the same inspector that wanted the light closed in 1883, recommended that the light be reestablished and the board heeded his request.[65]

On February 17, 1888, the Lighthouse Board ordered the reestablishment of the Copper Harbor light-station. Despite four years of abandonment, the buildings remained in good condition and needed only slight repairs. Preparations for relighting the station began with the opening of navigation, and on May 19, 1888, *The Mining Journal* published the following notice to mariners:

> [O]n or about June 1 a fixed white, of the fourth order, will be reestablished in the tower of the Copper Harbor main light station . . . at a height of sixty-five feet above the level of the lake, and should be seen in clear weather from the deck of a vessel ten feet above the lake fourteen and one-half statute miles.[66]

On May 22 Copper Harbor range lightkeeper Charles Davis recorded in his journal that "Mr. C., Lampist came . . . today to set up lens in the Main light." It is likely that he installed a 265 degree Fourth Order lens fully equipped with pedestal, service table, and lamps.

The light was relit on June 1 and Lighthouse Service crews maintained the station until the arrival of the keeper, Henry Corgan, on June 6. Corgan, the son of former Copper Harbor lightkeeper Charles Corgan, had requested a transfer from Peninsula Point, near Escanaba, Michigan, when he learned the light was going to be reestablished. Under Corgan's care a few repairs and renovations took place at the lighthouse, but it remained largely unchanged. He was the last Copper Harbor lightkeeper, serving for thirty-one years until the light was automated in 1919.

CHAPTER 3
WORK AND LIFE AT THE COPPER HARBOR LIGHTHOUSE

The job of painting, polishing, scouring, scrubbing, and swabbing is eternal.

Adamson — *Keepers of the Lights*

Many people view the position of lightkeepers as romantic and peaceful, but their lives are best described as routine, isolated, and monotonous. This section describes what it was like to work and live at a light-station situated on the remote Keweenaw Peninsula. Eight men served as keeper of the Copper Harbor light for nearly seventy years. Half of them were immigrants from Germany, Ireland and Canada. The original light was well maintained by keepers Henry Clow (1849-53), Henry Shurter (1853-55), and Napoleon Beedon (1855-69). Other keepers included John Power (1869-1873), Charles Corgan (1873-81), Edward Chambers (1881-1882), James W. Rich (1882-1883), and Henry Corgan (1888-1919). All shared the same experiences of isolation on the point, the duties of tending the light, and feelings of anxiety over the arrival of the district inspector.

Appointment, compensation and work at a lighthouse

In the early years of lighthouse administration the United States Secretary of the Treasury appointed keepers, one to each light, unless the light required an assistant. Before the creation of the Lighthouse Board in 1852, the Secretary of Treasury hired lightkeepers on the recommendation of local politicians. These men often rewarded their supporters with jobs. Eventually, standards were set that generally included an interview and nomination from the district collector of customs. Keepers were generally between the ages of eighteen and fifty, literate, able to keep accounts, and capable of manual labor. They also possessed some skill at minor repairs, such as painting or keeping the grounds in good order.

In the 1870s the Lighthouse Board began to make appointments and promotion of keepers strictly on merit, and nominees were placed on a three-month probation and employed as "acting keeper." Candidates then had to pass an examination before they could be given a "permanent appointment."[1] Many keepers transferred from lighthouse to lighthouse gradually rising in rank. While not a hereditary position, it was common for several generations of a family to serve as keepers, and many men (and a few women) had long distinguished careers with the Lighthouse Service. At Copper Harbor Charles Corgan and his son Henry served as keepers for a total of 39 years. Corgan's oldest son James worked at Gull Rock, Manitou Island, and the Ontonagon lights for over fifty years. One Copper Harbor range lightkeeper, Charles Davis, served for 45 years from 1885 to 1930.

Lighthouse regulations recognized only one rank of keeper's pay, but compensation was based on the length of service and the type of light-station operated. Obviously, at stations with more than one keeper assistants were paid less because they were subordinates. Pay was moderate at best, but keepers could live comfortably on their wages. In 1849 Henry Clow, the first keeper at Copper Harbor, received $350 per year, or $29.17 per month. In 1867 the government fixed the average wage of lightkeepers at $600 per year, yet the keeper at the main light at Copper Harbor received $560 and the range lightkeeper $400 per year because they worked nine months out of twelve.[2] Keepers were provided living quarters, land for gardens, and received fuel and lighthouse supplies. Still, many keepers often requested a pay increase to cover food and supply expenses. At Manitou Island, located off the tip of the Keweenaw, Angus McLoud Smith asked for an increase of $50 to cover the expense of having goods brought out to his station. The government granted his request because "propellers or other vessels very rarely stop at this Island and all the supplies for the keeper's family are charged double rates ... in addition to the amount charged on every article which is sent him from Detroit."[3]

In 1924 the Lighthouse Service continued to pay keepers based on the type of light-station they operated, but they set up a strict system of classifying stations. The system consisted of four classes based on the size of the illuminating apparatus, whether the stations had a fog signal, and the type of fog signal. Before the invention of fog horns, the service fitted light-stations with bells to warn vessels of danger. The first steam fog horn on the Keweenaw Peninsula was installed at Manitou Island in the 1880s, but the keepers at Copper Harbor operated hand fog horns. A Class 1 Station consisted of a watched station of minor importance (less than Fourth order fixed light without a fog signal), and base pay for an inexperienced man was $1,320. A Class 2 Station, like the Copper Harbor main and range lights, consisted of a manned lighthouse with a Fourth order light and fog signal of "less importance of that required for steam or air power." Pay at this station ranged from $1,380 to $1,620. A keeper at a Class 3 Station (without important fog signal) was paid between $1,440 and $1,680. The highest paid keepers worked at Class 4 stations, those of "primary importance" (with steam or air powered fog signals) and were paid between $1,500 and $1,740. The service granted an additional $60 per year for "moderate isolation," $120 for "extreme isolation," and $180 for "exceptional isolation, remoteness, and inaccessibility."[4] At Copper Harbor the keepers received no additional pay because their stations were less isolated and could be easily supplied by lighthouse tenders.

Before the installation of the Fresnel lens, keepers received limited instruction about their duties. One supervisor wrote that trimming and cleaning a small Argand fountain lamp was so simple that maintenance was "safely left to the intelligence" of the keeper.[5] Still, men new to the task of lightkeeping probably received some instruction from the outgoing keeper or trained at a nearby station. In 1893, Copper Harbor range lightkeeper Davis wrote that John Nolan, the newly appointed keeper at Gull Rock, trained and worked for two weeks at his station before heading out to "the rock."[6]

Beginning in 1852, the Lighthouse Board sent keepers detailed printed *Instructions* to ensure that keepers performed their duties correctly. The book left nothing to the keeper's imagination and covered all aspects of cleaning and maintaining the lantern, lamps, wicks, and lantern room. It also provided directions on outdoor work and preparing reports and daily logs. The board's 1870 *Instructions And Directions To Guide Light-House Keepers And Others Belonging To The Light-House Establishment* was 151 pages long. It began with set of 38 instructions concerning stations with one keeper and 27 instructions for stations with two or more keepers. Most of the pages detailed how to perform duties, attend the lighting apparatus, manage the lens and lamps, and test the oil; it also dictated what a keeper could expect as to the distribution of annual supplies.[7] If keepers followed these instructions, maintaining the light and grounds were relatively routine tasks.

In later years the Lighthouse Board published additional works specifically designed for training keepers of lighthouses and lightships. These included *Lighthouse Establishment Instructions; Instructions for the Management of Lenses; Lights and Beacons*; and *Management of Lens Apparatus and Lamps*. Beginning in 1869 the keeper also received an annual copy of the *Light List*, which furnished information regarding lighthouses, lighted beacons, lightships, buoys, and fog signals throughout the country.[8] The list included the name of each navigational aid, the character and period of the light, location and height of the structure, the distance seen in clear weather, and the approximate candlepower of the light.

The main task of the keeper, obviously, was to provide a light for the mariner to see from sunset to sunrise. The Copper Harbor light did not have an assistant keeper so the duties rested on one man. At stations with assistant keepers, however, they divided the duties into two compartments. When tending the light, the keeper usually rose at sunrise and would go into the oil room and measure the amount needed to fill the lamp. He then put on his linen apron (required when entering the lantern), picked up his oil kit, and entered the lantern to extinguish the light. Upon entering the lantern he slowly lowered the wick in the lamp and blew out the light, afterwards checking his watch so he could record the time of day that the light was extinguished. When tending the wick, he used trimming scissors to remove burned portions and rubbed off the excess with his thumb to make the wick level. If a wick needed replacement the burner was removed and a new wick put in with the aid of the wick mandrel. After tending the wicks he went on to clean the reservoirs, tubes, and burners of the lamp. Once every two weeks the burners and lamps were cleaned in "hot lye" or soap and water to remove charred and gummy residue. Oil from the night before was poured from the reservoir into a container and set aside to cool, and then filtered for use in hand and house lamps and cleaning brass work and utensils. Depending on the temperature, the keeper filled the oil reservoir with fresh, clean oil, but if the oil needed reheating, he waited until relighting in the evening so the oil would not congeal in the lamp. After tending the wicks and lantern the keeper covered the lamps and burners with cloth, and then prepared the interior and exterior of the lantern for lighting that night. Regulations required that the above duties be completed before ten o'clock in the morning for relighting in the evening.

Besides taking care of the lamps, wicks and oil, keepers had other duties. These included cleaning the copper and brass fixtures of the apparatus and utensils associated with the lantern room, plus washing the walls, floors, balconies, tower stairway, doors, windows, passageways, and oil storage area. They also filled out paperwork, such as daily journals and supply forms.[9]

Keepers were required to use materials supplied by the government for repair, cleaning, and polishing the lantern and lenticular apparatus. Soft materials were used to prevent scratching or damaging lighthouse fixtures. For example, when cleaning the lantern they used rouge powder on plate glass and polished brass with "buff" or chamois skins. Other cleaning materials consisted of whiting, spirits of wine, and linen cleaning cloths. The Lighthouse Service also gave keepers a complete set of tools for maintaining the lantern. Their tool boxes were equipped with files, hammers, levels, lucerenes, nippers, pliers, rulers, scrapers, and screw drivers.

The men and women who watched the lights performed many odd jobs around the lighthouse. Work on the buildings consisted of roof and foundation repair, replacement of doors, floors, windows and shutters, and extensive replastering and painting. Painting remained one of the more arduous tasks, and as early as 1870 the board required that specific paints be used for interior and exterior parts of the tower, lantern, and exterior of the building. *Instructions* stated that white be used exclusively for painting the interior of lighthouse lanterns, with the exterior of the lantern, including balustrades, railings, cowl, and ventilators painted black or red. The board strictly prohibited changing the outside color of the building without authorization. Around 1900 paint schemes became more regulated, as the board specified which colors to use for the entire structure. On the outside of the building the keepers used dark red, brown, or white for exposed wood, red or lead color for trim, black for the lantern and gallery railings, and red,

The U.S. Lighthouse Service provided lightkeepers with tools and materials to maintain their station. Lighthouse keepers spent much of their time repairing windows, doors and lamps.

green, or brown for shutters. The keeper also whitewashed stone, brick, and rough board work when authorized by the district inspector. Inside colors consisted of white for the interior of the lantern, walls, cellars, outhouses, and all woodwork except hardwood. Pine and hardwood floors were generally left unpainted and kept "well oiled and scrubbed." Green paints were used on pedestals and work tables, and gray on floors, staircases, and walls when authorized. Black was the primary color for iron staircases, railings, and interior ironwork, and black or white paint was used on the underside of tower stairways.[10]

Weather, of course, determined the work done at lighthouses. With about 250 inches of snow annually, the Keweenaw Peninsula gets more than its share of severe weather. The winter season typically begins in October and continues until May (with snow four feet deep and drifts ten feet high). During snow squalls the keeper kept a keen watch for vessels near his station. Some stations had ice problems which required the keeper to check the light to make sure it worked properly, and many times they removed ice and snow that covered the lantern.

If a vessel was in distress, the keeper used any means possible to be of assistance and routinely rescued mariners in nearby waters. Obviously, they used discretion when boating out on Lake Superior during severe storms. On July 27, 1901, the *Cigar*, fully loaded with iron ore, ran ashore about three miles east of Copper Harbor. Main lightkeeper Henry Corgan heard the ship's distress signal, launched his boat, and brought the captain back to get assistance.[11] During a storm on October 20, 1923, the steamer *Mather* went ashore about eight miles east of Copper Harbor. In an attempt to get word to the owners of the vessel, two members of her crew walked the shoreline and reached the range lighthouse exhausted and unable to go any farther. Accordingly, keeper Charles Davis "got them a meal and gave them a bed," and then left for Calumet (36 miles distant) to deliver the message himself. For his assistance Davis received a commendation from the Commissioner of Lighthouses.[12]

Rainy days called for indoor work and completing paperwork headed the list. The work load consisted of monthly, quarterly, and annual reports of supplies expended and received, reports of absences, the number of passing vessels, and, when necessary, shipwreck reports. These accounts were sent to the district inspector and forwarded to the Lighthouse Board at Washington, D.C. Keepers also kept a journal showing the daily expenditure of oil, wicks, chimneys, and the state of the weather during the exhibition of the light. They particularly noticed severe and unpredictable weather. On June 14, 1875, the range lightkeeper observed: "Channel fild [sic] with ice. No boat could come in," and on May 10, 1891, he wrote, "95 in shade on the 8th instant, and snow this evening."[13] Outdoor chores could be unbearable for the climate, and the verdant forests of the Keweenaw

Strict rules and regulations governed the lightkeeper's work. Beginning in 1852, the Lighthouse Board gave keepers printed instructions for tending their stations. Along with other duties, keepers kept a daily journal, filed reports and made sure the light worked at all times.

provided excellent breeding ground for insects. Mosquitoes, black flies and other bugs were bothersome throughout the summer months. One keeper lamented, "The black flies [are] so bad that it was almost impossible to work."[14]

As a supplement to their yearly food ration, the government encouraged lightkeepers to try their hands at gardening to supply fresh vegetables. Since the eastern point of Copper Harbor consisted of conglomerate and trap rock with almost no soil, the keeper there did not keep a garden. However, the soil on the opposite side of the harbor proved productive so range lightkeeper Davis kept a garden next to the house and at his farm near the village. On June 13, 1893, he recorded in his journal that he had "set out tomato plants, carrots, onions, peas, [and] rutabagas."

Besides their everyday duties, Copper Harbor lightkeepers looked after the buildings at Fort Wilkins. Built in 1844, Fort Wilkins was occupied by federal troops during the "copper rush." In 1846 the troops were transferred to the southern border to fight in the Mexican War. Briefly reoccupied by Civil War veterans from 1867-1870, the U.S. Army permanently abandoned the fort in August 1870. Except for a brief period in the 1880s, the main lightkeeper served as custodian of the fort property from October 1870 to August 1900 without additional compensation. On April 19, 1892, the War Department transferred Lots 2 and 3 of Section 33, consisting of Fort Wilkins, to the Lighthouse Board. At this time, range lightkeeper Davis was placed in charge of the fort because he lived closer to it and was better able to look after the buildings. Davis served as caretaker until Fort Wilkins was sold to Houghton and Keweenaw Counties in 1921.[15]

The Lighthouse Service scheduled periodic visits to light-stations, and the inspector would travel three times a year to examine lights within his district. Inspections followed a steady routine that began when the ship arrived. First, the keeper would greet the supply party at the dock, and after the formalities report on the amount of oil on hand and the number of oil cases that needed recycling. The Lighthouse Board reused oil canisters and methodically recorded the date when the case was emptied, the name of the light-station, and the condition of the canister upon return. Second, the inspection party went to the dwelling and looked at the account books while the keeper presented all worn out supplies, such as paint brushes, brooms, mops, broken tools, etc. All supplies in poor condition were replaced on the spot, with worn out supplies taken aboard the supply tender for repair or disposal at the district headquarters. Finally, the keeper recorded all new supplies into the supply and expenditure books. If tools or equipment were lost due to carelessness, keepers were held responsible and had to pay out of pocket for a replacement. Unannounced visits were common, and until the invention of the telephone keepers typically had

Lightkeeper Charles T. Davis (shown here about 1890) served as the Copper Harbor range lightkeeper for 45 years, from 1885 to 1930.

no idea when the inspector would arrive. On June 10, 1890, Copper Harbor range lightkeeper Davis noted that the inspector was "perfectly satisfied" with the condition of his station. But Davis' attitude changed a few years later when he lamented, "I have been on the sick list this morning and had not cleaned the lantern windows when the Inspector came ashore. I received a reprimand in consequence."[16]

Like any other employer the Lighthouse Board felt the anxiety of keeping trained and experienced people. A lightkeeper's position became vacant if the keeper died, resigned, or was dismissed by the Lighthouse Board. Prior to examinations, district inspectors fired keepers if they were found intoxicated or failed to keep their light burning. In 1893 the Lighthouse Board reported that vacancies caused by death were "inconsiderable in number," and that just one in seven new keepers received notice of removal. Resignations remained the main cause for the loss of employees with five or six of every seven quitting the service. For example, between 1885 and 1889 the board hired 1,190 new keepers, and 680 of these, or 57%, resigned their positions. Still, the board insisted that low pay was not the primary cause for vacancy, since only 120 (10%) of those who resigned left the service because of low pay.[17] Similarly, of the twenty-seven keepers who worked at Copper Harbor (both stations), Gull Rock, and Manitou Island lights from 1848-1888, eight (27%) of the keepers resigned and seven (26%) were removed.[18] Many keepers probably resigned their positions due to the isolation of their stations, for Gull Rock and Manitou Island are situated off the tip of the peninsula.

On May 1, 1884, to establish the image of a career service and a sense of pride among the ranks of lighthouse keepers, the board issued regulation uniforms for the first time. The government gave current employees their first uniform, but after that date keepers had to purchases their own uniforms. It consisted of a coat, vest, trousers, and a cap made of "dark indigo-blue kersey or flannel." The double-breasted coat had five large regulation buttons on each side (complete with two small buttons on the cuff of each sleeve). The uniform also had a single breasted vest without a collar, and three pockets with five small regulation buttons. Keeper's pants were cut in the prevailing style of the period. The cap, finished with an attached yellow metal lighthouse badge, had an adjustable chin strap held in place by regulation buttons.[19] Accordingly, keepers wore their uniform during inspections or on special days when they expected visitors, but when they painted or performed messy chores they put on the prescribed working suit (typically brown or white coveralls).

Besides promoting a sense of pride the government also took steps to promote efficiency and friendly rivalry among its keepers. In 1912 keepers who served with distinction during quarterly inspections were allowed to wear the "Inspectors's Star" for the next year. The star, a simple decorated pin, was worn on the keeper's uniform. Those who received the star for three successive years received the "Commissioner's Star." Besides these pins the efficiency pennant, or Lighthouse Service flag, was awarded annually to the best light-station in each district. The winning station had bragging rights and would fly the flag for an entire year.[20]

Life at a lighthouse

The isolation of many light-stations affected the keeper's life more than anything else. Lighthouses on Lake Superior were more remote than stations on other lakes because of their location, the distance between lights, and the severe climate. Keepers at Copper Harbor fared better than other places on Lake Superior, for they could row across the harbor or walk the narrow three mile trail to the village. The keepers at Manitou Island and Gull Rock, however, sailed out to their lights when the ice began to break in the spring and remained there until the close of the shipping season. Although trips ashore were infrequent, lightkeepers visited the mainland to get supplies, fuel, and mail. Lake travel to and from the mainland by boat could be dangerous, as Gull Rock keeper James Corgan described during a gale on September 8, 1877:

> Left Copper Harbor for Gull Rock at 3 PM.... at 7:15 heavy sea, wind light SE. Started to sail across to Light House[,] wind freshened [and] was heavily loaded and boat leaked bad ... came very near to swamping within half a mile of Light house [and] had to turn back to mainland. After two hours of unsuccessful sailing to get to Gull Rock, I came nearer to being lost than I ever was since I first entered the Light-House Service.... I landed on long beach and lost my rudder, got boat into shelter and remained for the night.

The next day Corgan repaired his boat and waited until the wind died down. After a miserable trip he arrived at his station at 3:30 that afternoon, "tired, hungry and weary."[21]

Depending on the accessibility, location, and importance of stations, the government hired assistants to help maintain aids to navigation. At important light-stations with steam powered fog horns and first through third order lights, there were two to five keepers, including one assistant who served as the steam engineer. Generally, pierhead or harbor lights (like Copper Harbor) did not have an assistant keeper. At some isolated stations as many as four men served as assistants, but the Gull Rock and Manitou Island stations had one and two assistants respectively. Regulations prohibited the employment of women to manage lights unless they had some previous connection with the lights they served, like being widows or daughters of keepers. The Lighthouse Service could be reasonable, however, when circumstances called for the appointment of women. In 1897 John Nolan, keeper at Gull Rock, asked that his wife be allowed to live

Each lighthouse district maintained a depot and a supply tender which brought food, fuel and repair crews to light-stations. Shown here is the tender *Marigold* at Copper Harbor on July 15, 1915.

with him during the summer months at that station. At first the service denied the request, but when the assistant transferred they appointed his wife to fill the vacancy.

The government supplied lighthouses with nearly every item needed to keep the station operating. Before 1860 all fuel and supplies came from New Bedford, Connecticut. With the adoption of lard oil as the primary fuel, Staten Island, New York, became the central supply depot for the entire country. Materials and supplies from New York were shipped to district depots. More than just storage facilities, these depots included landing docks and carpenter, machine and blacksmith shops for repairing the varied supplies for the service. These places also served as the headquarters and point of departure for supply ships.

Lighthouse supply ships, called "tenders," distributed goods to light-stations from district headquarters. During the 1890s, four tenders operated on the upper lakes: the *Marigold* and *Warrington* delivered supplies and provisions, while the *Amaranth* and *Lotus* transported the district engineer with construction and repair crews.[22] The *Marigold* and *Amaranth* operated well into the twentieth century and each carried a crew of six officers and about twenty men. As part of their duties supply crews purchased local foodstuffs, fuel, and construction material on the open market to provide supplies to light-stations on the Keweenaw. The government also contracted with local merchants to supply "fresh provisions" to all light-stations. Between 1880 and 1911 the stores of Smith and Harris and the Pure Food Company of Houghton provided goods for the Copper Harbor lights.[23] If keepers wanted to vary their table fare, they could buy other goods like fresh meats, vegetables or canned goods at their own expense.

Under special authority, the board granted isolated stations an annual allowance of provisions and food because they had limited access to mainland supplies and stores. On the Keweenaw Peninsula, keepers at Gull Rock and Manitou Island fell under this category. In 1881, these stations received 200 lbs. pork, 100 lbs. beef, 2 barrels flour, 50 lbs. rice, 50 lbs. brown sugar, 24 lbs. coffee, 10 gallons beans or peas, 4 gallons of vinegar, and 2 barrels of potatoes per man.[24] To help stop spoilage, the Lighthouse Service often packed supplies in sturdy wooden barrels or kegs.

Naturally, isolated stations received a greater number and variety of supplies than those near villages and cities. When comparing the lists of *Supplies Received and Consumed* at the Gull Rock and Copper Harbor light-stations many additional supplies are evident at the former site. Gull Rock lightkeepers received more utilitarian articles such as screen doors, storm sashes, kettles, frying and stove pans, and stove pipes for the galley. They also received extra beeswax, caulking tools, oar locks, sewing accessories, and masts to repair its sailboat. The Lighthouse Service could be more generous with miscellaneous articles as well, supplying the Gull Rock station with a library, a row boat, oars, glass polish, and a spare hand-operated fog horn. Finally, if the keepers

The lighthouse service supplied keepers with nearly everything they needed to keep their station operative. Annual food rations, like pork, rice, beans and coffee, changed little during the 70 years the Copper Harbor light was manned.

were sick or injured, they had access to a medicine chest and medical book complete with instructions for treating sprains and broken bones.

To compensate for isolation the Lighthouse Service began to issue libraries. Reading material could help pass long and lonely hours at distant stations. First introduced in 1876, they originated out of the need to satisfy the "intellectual requirement" of keepers. At first the libraries were left at stations for six months, but as their popularity grew they were eventually exchanged about every three months. Early on they collected fifty libraries, but by the 1880s more than 500 were in circulation. These libraries consisted of a pine box two feet high by two feet wide, packed with about 35 to 40 books. Each library had a different mixture of history, fiction, scientific, and religious works along with a few magazines.[25] Although no record has been found showing that the Copper Harbor lights received one of these libraries, no doubt the keepers appreciated new reading material. In 1891 Copper Harbor range lightkeeper Charles Davis wrote that "Mr. Frank Scott... brought a bundle of newspapers and magazines which we were very thankful to receive, as reading material is a scarce article..." Besides reading, other recreational activities included hunting, fishing, berrying, mail-order courses, collecting stamps, and excursions to mining locations like Delaware, Calumet, and Portage Lake.

At stations where the keeper had a family, the education of children was a major problem. The Lighthouse Board attempted to place keepers with families at stations near towns and villages, but parents often had to serve as teachers. At isolated lighthouses, many keepers attempted to transfer once their children reached school age. In 1874 Stephen Cocking, keeper at Gull Rock, wrote:

> Having served six years at this lonely light station, which is 14 miles from any school and on a small barren rock I beg to be transferd [sic] to some station near a village or town in which there is a school so as to be able to educate my children.... by granting me this favor you will be doing my family a great service.[26]

The board granted his request and moved him to Eagle Harbor the next year. Keepers at Copper Harbor usually boarded their families in the village so their children could go the local school. On one occasion John Power, while serving as both the main lightkeeper and school teacher at Copper Harbor, decided to live in the village rather than at his station. When the board learned of his absence they informed him that he must live at the station or "send in his resignation." Power responded by moving back out to lighthouse.[27]

If someone watched the light, keepers could leave their stations to go to church, obtain supplies and attend important public events. At stations with more than one keeper at least one person had to maintain the light. No rules were established to limit the number or length of absences, but the government held the keeper accountable for abusing the privilege. At many lighthouses family members helped with the keeper's duties or looked after the light in his absence. In fact, this happened at Copper Harbor. Range lightkeeper Charles Davis frequently kept an eye on his counterpart across the harbor, and recorded several journal entries describing Henry Corgan's absence from his station. For example, on July 20, 1900, Corgan left for Houghton leaving "Charles Conkling and Emmit Corgan [his son] in charge of the light." Two years later keeper Corgan "left for Calumet" and young Emmit and his five-year-old sister Rosy "looked after the light."

Keepers were forbidden to engage in businesses that interfered with their lighthouse duties. Still, throughout the Lighthouse Service many keepers worked as school teachers, post masters or justices of the peace. At Copper Harbor Charles Corgan and his son Henry worked as "acting justices" of the peace, and John Power taught at the local school. Additionally, with permission from the Lighthouse Board, Henry Corgan and Charles Davis both operated a fishing business while stationed there. Perhaps Corgan left his station once too often for he faced charges for "neglect of duty to engage in private pursuits" in 1894. In July of that year the inspector traveled to Copper Harbor to investigate and recommended that "no action be taken" against the keeper.[28]

Despite mining activity on the Keweenaw Peninsula and the growth of communities farther south, Copper Harbor remained remote and sparsely populated. A few small copper mines operated nearby, but none were successful. In the 1870s and 1880s the harbor served as a refueling depot for vessels rounding Keweenaw Point, but little business took place. William Tresise, Copper Harbor range lightkeeper from 1870-1885, remarked on the isolation of his station, noting that "today is Sunday and loonsom [sic]. One man passed on horse back that[']s all."[29] Nevertheless, social calls were common at many lighthouses. When visitors arrived at a station, the keeper typically gave them a tour showing them the illuminating apparatus, buildings, and other objects of interest free of charge. Regulations stipulated that visitors could go into the tower only when accompanied by the keeper, and under no circumstances was an intoxicated person allowed near the station. Keepers and their families frequently visited local residents as well, as noted by the Copper Harbor range lightkeeper:

> Aug. 30, 1873
>   A social party was given at Copper Harbor. . . .
>   Myself and wife tended until twelve o'clock
> Aug. 18, 1877
>   I went to the Clark Mine today
> Oct. 1, 1885
>   Manito [sic] and Gull rock keepers came up
> Aug. 8, 1888
>   Mr. and Mrs. Corgan and children came over for a visit

National holidays and events were occasions of festivity at Copper Harbor, and Fort Wilkins served as a central gathering place more than once. In 1883, for example, range lightkeeper Tresise noted that "the other [main light] keeper and my self Deckerade [sic] the Fort for a dance and shooting mach [sic]." Local and national events were also attended by keepers. In 1893, main lightkeeper Henry Corgan and his

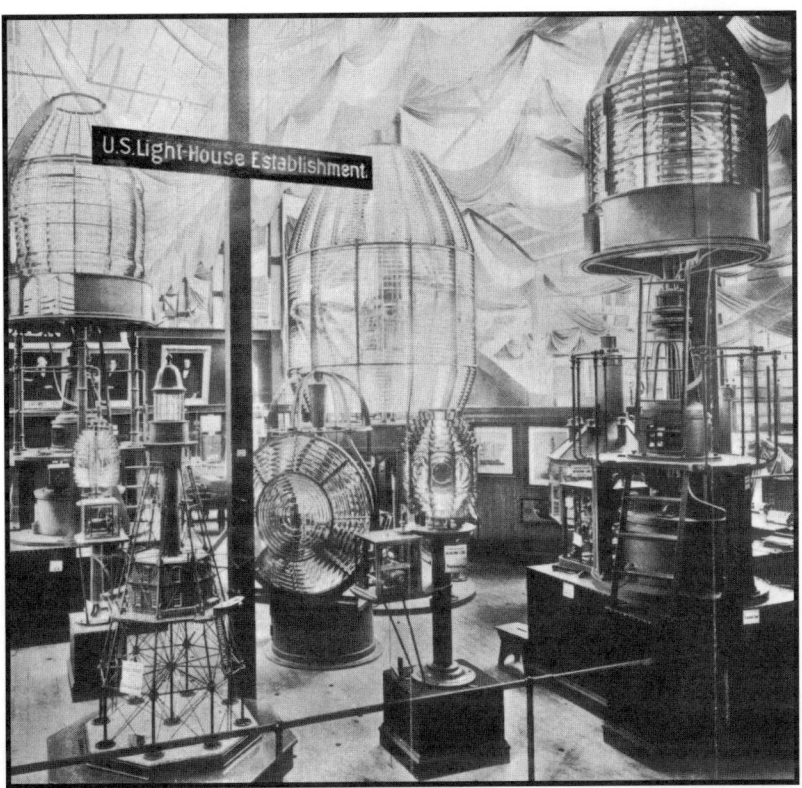

In 1893 the U.S. Lighthouse Establishment exhibited lenses, models, plans and photographs at the World's Columbian Exposition in Chicago, Illinois. Copper Harbor lightkeeper Henry Corgan and his daughter Molly were among the millions of tourists to see the fair.

daughter attended the Colombian Exhibition at the Chicago World's Fair, and in 1902 Charles Davis went to Calumet to see "Buffalo Bill's Wild West Show."[30]

The Copper Harbor lightkeepers shared many of the same experiences as their counterparts at other stations within the Lighthouse Service. Governmental regulations and instructions provided a strict regimen of daily routine that consisted of cleaning and maintaining the lantern, lighthouse, grounds, and completing paperwork such as monthly, quarterly, and annual reports. Still, their primary responsibility was maintaining a good light for the mariner to see from sunset to sunrise.

Copper Harbor Lightkeepers[31]

Henry Clow, 1849-1853

Henry Clow was born in Germany and arrived in the United States around 1837. His U.S. military record showed that he enlisted in Company A, 5th Infantry at Jefferson Barracks, Missouri, on April 13, 1841. Clow served at Detroit before being transferred to Copper Harbor in May of 1844, where he was stationed at Fort Wilkins until August of 1845. While there he worked as a cooper and helped with the construction of the garrison. With the threat of war with Mexico, in 1846 Company A was transferred to Corpus Cristi, Texas. Clow participated in the Mexican War until discharged on April 15, 1846, at Point Isabella, Texas.[32]

After his discharge Henry Clow returned to the Keweenaw Peninsula, and on February 24, 1849, was appointed the first lightkeeper at Copper Harbor. He earned $350 per year until he resigned on August 5, 1853.[33]

Henry Shurter, 1853-1855

On August 5, 1853, James Guthrie, the Secretary of Treasury, appointed Henry Shurter as keeper of the Copper Harbor lighthouse for $350 per year, or about $29 per month. Shurter's tenure as keeper was short, as he was dismissed on March 23, 1855. The grounds for his dismissal are unknown.

Napoleon Beedon, 1855-1869

Napoleon Bonaparte Beedon was born on March 29, 1836, at Whitmore Lake, Michigan, the second of eight children born to John and Martha Ann Beedon. In 1846 his father, John Beedon, moved the family to L'Anse, Michigan, so he could work for the government as an "Indian Farmer" at the Catholic Mission near the head of Keweenaw Bay. In April of 1849 his son Napoleon was employed as the assistant blacksmith at the farm. While there Napoleon lost an arm in an accident.[34]

In 1851 Beedon's father moved his family north so he could work as the manager of the Iron City Copper Mine, located five miles from Copper Harbor. On March 23, 1855, Napoleon Beedon was appointed as Copper Harbor lighthouse keeper. He served for fourteen years until his resignation on September 9, 1869. While living at Copper Harbor he married Mary Hickey, a native of Waterford, Ireland, on September 29, 1859.35

Napoleon Bonaparte Beedon, shown here at a later age, served as Copper Harbor lightkeeper from 1855 to 1869.

After he resigned as keeper at Copper Harbor Napoleon moved his family to Munising, Michigan. Apparently he enjoyed working for the Lighthouse Service, for he served at the East Channel and Grand Island Harbor lights between December 7, 1870, and May 6, 1876. On July 6, 1876, he transferred to the Big Sable (Au Sable) lighthouse located between Whitefish Point and Grand Island Harbor. While there his wife was appointed as his assistant at $420 per year, thus adding the name Beedon to the list of husband and wife teams to serve as lightkeepers on Lake Superior. Beedon and his wife resigned their positions on July 19, 1879. In his last entry as a lightkeeper he wrote:

> N. Beedon has been in the employ of the government for 28 years and has resigned twice during that time. I have been instrumental in Saving Many

a person from a watery grave.... I have cleared up many an acre of land for the government [having] cleared 5 different light House Stations that I have found in a state of wilderness.36

Napoleon Beedon moved to Ashland, Wisconsin, and resided there until his death on January 11, 1913, at the age of seventy-seven.

John Power, 1869-1873

John Power was born July 13, 1846, in Waterford, Ireland, the fifth of nine children born to Matthew Power and Bridget Veale Power. Power attended Waterford public schools before immigrating to America in 1863. When he arrived at New York he enlisted with Company A, 17th New York Volunteers, for a term of three years to fight in the Civil War. His enlistment record shows that he was dark complected and had hazel eyes, and was five feet eight inches in height.37 In September 1864, Power was wounded at the Battle of Hatcher's Run, Virginia. In August of 1865 he reenlisted in Company E, 18th U.S. Infantry, Veterans Reserve Corps (VRC) and deserted his unit on November 27, 1865. The reason for his desertion is unknown, but on May 17, 1867, he enlisted again with Company E, 43rd Infantry at Chicago. That summer his unit transferred to Fort Wayne, Detroit, where he climbed the enlisted ranks to corporal on July 1, then sergeant on September 10. His unit was then transferred to Fort Wilkins and arrived at Copper Harbor on the night of September 24, 1867. Power served as a first sergeant at Fort Wilkins until his discharge under Surgeon's Certificate of Disability on April 8, 1869.38

While stationed at the fort in September 1868, John Power married Elizabeth Corgan, the daughter of Manitou Island lightkeeper Charles Corgan of Copper Harbor. They remained at Copper Harbor after his discharge from the Army, and on September 1, 1869, he was appointed keeper of the Copper Harbor lighthouse. As part of his duties he was appointed caretaker of Fort Wilkins when the U.S. Army left in October 1870, and as compensation he was permitted to use the fort garden and live in one of the fort buildings during the winter months. He served as lightkeeper until his resignation on July 25, 1873, earning $560 per year.

During his stay at Copper Harbor, Power was hired to teach primary school from November 1, 1869 until July 1873. The school paid him $55 per month, but during the final two years he received $70 per month. Moreover, during this period Power found time to study law and was admitted to the Michigan Bar in 1872.

A former soldier at Fort Wilkins, John Power served as the Copper Harbor lightkeeper from 1869 to 1873. He later became a successful Upper Peninsula educator, politician and lawyer.

During the late 1870s John Power moved his family to Red Jacket, Michigan, and opened a law office. While there he won the Democratic nomination for the office of Keweenaw County Prosecutor and for a time served as the village attorney. In 1881 Power moved to Escanaba, Michigan, where he became a "versatile trial lawyer and a skilled . . . counselor." He continued to pursue politics and was nominated as the district delegate to the Democratic National Convention in 1884, 1892, and 1904.[39]

Power continued his interest in education serving as a member and president of the Escanaba Board of Education, and serving as county superintendent of schools for ten years. Considered a "man of high ideals and generous impulses" Power spent his later years in the real estate and insurance businesses. An ambitious and successful soldier, lawyer, and educator, Power's life was aptly summarized by one author who wrote: "the life of John Power shows what may be accomplished by an intelligent and industrious boy in America. Coming here without money or influential friends, he had steadily worked his way upward."[40] In 1920, while visiting relatives, John Power passed away at Chicago, Illinois, at the age of seventy-four.

Charles Corgan, 1873-1881

Born in Ireland in 1820 Charles Corgan came to North America with his wife, Mary Mooney Corgan, in 1842. They resided at Montreal until 1864, where he taught school, farmed, and manufactured lumber for the Canadian Government for its road building program. In 1864 the Corgan family migrated to the Keweenaw Peninsula and moved to Copper Harbor, where he found employment with the Clark Copper Mining Company.[41] On July 10, 1866, he was appointed as lighthouse keeper at Manitou Island when keeper Edwin Bennett resigned. While serving at Manitou his three sons, Hugh, James, and Henry, worked as his assistants.

Corgan was appointed as acting keeper at Copper Harbor on October 21, 1873, and received his permanent appointment on November 11, 1876, at a salary of $560 per year. Why the Lighthouse Board did not grant Corgan a permanent appointment until three years had passed is unknown, since it was common practice during the 1870s to have only a three month trial period.

The June 1870 Census lists Charles Corgan as "Govt. Lighthouse Keeper" with his personal estate valued at $700. Charles, age 50 in 1870, and his wife Mary (46) had six children; James (23), Sarah (17), Henry (15), Mary (13), Daniel (12), and Nellie (10). Corgan served as Director of the School Board in

1870, Treasurer in 1873, and Moderator in 1875. Active in civil affairs he also worked as justice of the peace from November 3, 1874, to July 4, 1878, and again in 1881 and 1884.[42]

Besides his everyday duties as lighthouse keeper, Corgan also served as caretaker of the buildings at Fort Wilkins without additional compensation until 1881. After nine years as keeper at Copper Harbor light he was removed on October 5, 1881. The circumstances of his removal are unknown, but the government probably dismissed him for leaving the light unattended or found intoxicated while on duty.[43] The Lighthouse Service acted swiftly to find a replacement, and they nominated Edward Chambers on November 11. One month later Chambers transferred from Whitefish Point to Copper Harbor to serve as lighthouse keeper. Corgan remained at Copper Harbor after his dismissal as keeper and tried his luck as a hotel keeper during the mid 1880s. As one of the early residents and public leaders of Copper Harbor, Charles Corgan gained the reputation as "a highly respected man, [often] winning friends wherever he went."[44] Charles Corgan suffered heart problems and died at the lighthouse while visiting his son on May 2, 1889. He is buried in the Copper Harbor cemetery.

A native of Ireland, Charles Corgan first worked as lightkeeper at Manitou Island before transferring to Copper Harbor. He served at Copper Harbor for nine years and later operated a hotel in the village.

Edward Chambers and James W. Rich, 1881-1883

Edward Chambers was born on January 9, 1852, at Mackinac, Michigan. Before entering the Lighthouse Service on May 25, 1878, he worked as a sailor on the Great Lakes. Where he first worked as lightkeeper is unknown, but prior to his appointment at Copper Harbor he served at the Whitefish Point lighthouse. Described as a "faithful" and competent man, he served at Copper Harbor for one year until being transferred back to Whitefish Point on October 10, 1882.

Chambers worked at several light-stations including Round Island, St. Mary's River Range light, Point Iroquois, Stannard Rock, and Windmill Point stations. Interestingly, he served at Stannard Rock for twelve years, one of the most isolated stations on the Great Lakes. Overall, Edward Chambers served for 32 years with the Lighthouse Service. He died on July 17, 1910, at the age of 58.

James W. Rich served the shortest length of time as Copper Harbor lightkeeper. Rich was stationed at Cheyboygan, Michigan, prior to his appointment at Copper Harbor on November 8, 1882. He held the position of acting keeper until August 3, 1883, when he was appointed permanent lightkeeper, at a rate of $560 annually. Rich served at Copper Harbor until the light was discontinued on October 6, 1883. He then worked at Gull Rock for two years, and then moved to Grosse Point, Michigan in 1885.

Henry Corgan, 1888-1919

Henry Corgan was born on June 10, 1853, in Vaughn Township, Canada, the third of six children born to Charles Corgan and Mary Mooney Corgan. In 1864, at age eleven, he arrived in the Keweenaw Peninsula from Montreal, Canada, and spent his adolescent years in the village of Copper Harbor. He was educated at the Copper Harbor school and for a time was taught by his brother-in-law John Power, a former soldier at Fort Wilkins. On January 11,

1878, Henry married Catherine Dunn, age twenty-four, at Copper Harbor. The marriage record showed that Henry worked as a carpenter at this time.[45]

Henry Corgan first entered the Lighthouse Service as assistant keeper at Manitou Island following the resignation of his brother James on September 21, 1868. From there Corgan transferred, but when and where he moved is unknown. It is likely that he left the Lighthouse Service when his father transferred to Copper Harbor in October 1873, for his brother James and wife Mary were keeper and assistant keeper on Manitou Island from 1873 to 1875.

Corgan and his wife lived at Red Jacket (Calumet) in 1880 and 1881, residing at First Street. He worked as the village night watchman when the shipping season prevented him from tending the light. In 1883, Corgan moved back to Copper Harbor and operated a fishing business. Corgan, along with his wife and young son Henry Jr. (age 5½ months), boarded Charles Fox, a "cook/servant," and John Nolan, a "fisherman," in their home. Nolan, a longtime family friend, later served as Gull Rock lightkeeper from 1888 to 1903. Corgan invested $200 in the fishery and employed three males (over the age of sixteen) at full time for six months of the year. The total value of his operation, including "boats, nets, and fish," was $900.

Henry Corgan entered the Lighthouse Service on a continuous basis on December 29, 1885, when he took the oath as assistant keeper at Gull Rock. He gained permanent appointment on September 11, 1886, and served under keeper Norman Guilbault until his transfer to Peninsula Point Lighthouse, near Escanaba, Michigan, on March 12, 1887. While at Escanaba he learned of the relighting of the Copper Harbor light and wrote to the Secretary of the Lighthouse Board on June 23, 1888:

> I take the liberty of writing to you about the Copper Harbor Light. I formerly kept light at Copper Harbor

and was transferred from there to the Point Peninsula. Now my light is so situated that I am unable to send my children to school and in addition to that my wife does not enjoy good health here.... It would be a great favor for me to obtain the transfer. ... I have resided in Copper Harbor for 25 years, and have been in the Lt. House Service 10 years and this is the first favor I have asked during that length of time. I would be willing pay my own transfer expense providing I receive the appointment for Copper Harbor light.[46]

Corgan's statement that he had previously served as keeper at Copper Harbor doesn't make sense. His father Charles worked there from 1873 to 1881, Edward Chambers from 1881 to 1882, and James W. Rich kept the light until it closed in October 1883. It is possible that he may have helped his father with his duties during the 1870s. Whatever the case the Lighthouse Board granted the request, and on July 26, 1888, he arrived at Copper Harbor. The Corgan family resided in one of the buildings at Fort Wilkins during the winter months, for range lightkeeper Davis observed on November 20, 1888, and October 26, 1889, that the Corgan family had started "to move over" to the fort.[47]

Henry Corgan worked at the Copper Harbor lightstation for 31 years and was brought up on charges at least twice during this period. On June 16, 1894, William Smith, Copper Harbor Township Supervisor, wrote to Washington preferring charges against Corgan for "neglect of duty to engage in private pursuits" and being absent without leave. According to Smith, Corgan sent a number of people to watch the light, including his son and the local school children. Smith surmised that Corgan was at his station for about two days when the supply boat was there, it being "well known by him when said boat passes the Ste. Marie Canal." In late July the district inspector traveled to Copper

Harbor to investigate and determined that the charges should be dropped.[48] However, an examination of oil expenditure books for the Copper Harbor light showed that Smith's charges may have been true. In 1896 the only month Corgan left his signature was August, someone else had filled in the blanks for the remaining eight months.[49]

Two government "Efficiency Reports" provide insight into Corgan's abilities as a lightkeeper. These reports rated keepers based on quantity, quality and "interest manifested" in their work. A report dated June 5, 1909, shows that as part of his duties he was in charge of the light-station including custody of all public property on the reservation; keeping of the light; and preparation of all reports required by regulations. His evaluation rated him "fairly efficient," and he received a score of 80% for his work. In comparison his contemporary, Copper Harbor range lightkeeper Charles Davis, was rated "thoroughly efficient" and received a score of 100%. The 1911 efficiency report shows that Corgan's score had improved to 91%, yet Davis' score remained perfect.[50]

In 1919 the Lighthouse Service automated the Copper Harbor light and eliminated the need for a permanent keeper. The government offered Corgan a transfer to St. Clair Flats Canal Upper Light-Station, near Detroit. He worked there until he retired from active duty as lighthouse keeper on September 24, 1924, at the age of seventy-one. Henry Corgan died in Detroit on August 7, 1930.[51]

Government lightkeepers and their families manned the Copper Harbor light until 1919. This image shows the back of the lighthouse in 1913 (Note the barrel used to catch rain water from the gutters).

CHAPTER 4
EPILOGUE

During the 20th Century the Lighthouse Service began establishing automatic lights throughout the United States. The introduction of new fuels, like acetylene gas and electricity, lessened the cost of operation and offered better service to mariners by permitting flashing lights in place of fixed lights. The change in illuminant also provided many stations with an increase in candlepower, so lights could be seen at a greater distance. Thus, shipping on Lake Superior became much safer since vessels no longer had to hug the shoreline. The age of lighthouse keeping was coming to a close because keepers were no longer needed at stations where the light had been automated. Many stations were closed and eventually put up for sale.

In January of 1919 the government proposed to automate the Copper Harbor light. According to the Bureau of Lighthouses automation of the light would save the government $800 per year in maintenance "without a loss in efficiency." In addition to saving money the government had a place to transfer keeper Henry Corgan. The keeper at St. Clair Flats Canal Upper Light-Station, near Detroit, Michigan, was about to retire. Corgan made preparations to move and on March 24, 1919, he left for Detroit. The Copper Harbor main light-station was then placed under the charge of the range light-keeper, Charles Davis. Davis regularly checked the acetylene tanks, lighthouse, and grounds and for the extra work received an increase in pay from $780 to $840 per year.[1]

When the fuel was changed from mineral oil to acetylene gas, the characteristic of the Copper Harbor light also changed. The light was changed from fixed to flashing white every three seconds: light .3 seconds, eclipse 2.7 seconds. To fuel the light a small pilot flame burned continuously and ignited the charges of gas released by a flashing mechanism. Gas was stored in a tank at the base of the 1866 lighthouse tower and fitted with a one-foot burner that provided 470 candlepower, the same as it was before. The light could be seen at a distance of about fifteen miles during clear weather.[2] In the 1920s ship captains rounding Keweenaw Point had a difficult time distinguishing the lights at Copper Harbor, Eagle Harbor, and Manitou Island because they all had flashing white lights. In 1924 the board received several complaints and responded by changing the characteristic of the light at Copper Harbor to a flash of .3 second every second.[3]

In May 1932 the bureau ordered the construction of a steel tower to house the light, but due to a shortage of funds they put off the work until the following year. On May 5, 1933, Charles Park, Superintendent of Lighthouses, wanted the light moved to a 60-foot steel tower and pushed for the sale the land and buildings on the reservation. A plan was approved and the site for the new light was selected 77 feet (23 meters) west of the 1866 light tower, approximately the same location of the original 1848 stone tower.[4]

The steel tower's design called for a concrete foundation with four concrete footings. Each footing was four feet high and beveled on the top to form a square for the legs of the tower. Workers moved the wooden acetylene tank house from the front of the 1866 lighthouse and placed it directly under the steel tower. A 375mm acetylene lantern with a 1¼ inch burner was placed on the top of the steel tower. It showed the same characteristic of the old light (flashing), but it had an increase of 480 candlepower. The total cost of the project, including materials and labor, was $1,750. So mariners could distinguish the tower

During the early 1900s the government sought cheaper alternatives to fuel lighthouses. Longer burning fuels and electricity meant that keepers no longer needed to maintain the light every day. The Copper Harbor lighthouse was automated in 1919 and in 1933 the light was moved to a steel tower.

during the day, it was painted black, but in 1935 vessel owners complained that the tower was hard to see because it blended into the forest surrounding the lighthouse. As a fix the bureau painted the front of the 1866 lighthouse white to increase the tower's visibility.[5]

The Copper Harbor range light also received an overhaul in the 1930s. In order to increase the candlepower of the rear range, and to provide the keeper with utilities, the rear range light and dwelling were equipped with a 32-volt electric lighting plant in 1933.6 In 1937 the bureau planned to electrify the main light and at the same time change the Copper Harbor front range light from kerosene to electricity. According to F.P. Dillon, 11th District Superintendent, the range lighthouse was of minor importance and maintained for "aged and deserving keepers" who could not "perform more laborious duties" at more difficult stations. The range lightkeeper, Charles Haven, retired on July 1 and the Coast Guard changed the light's fuel from acetylene gas to electricity in November. The total cost of electrifying both stations was $1,060, and the government estimated an annual savings of $1,300. Work crews installed Edison zinc copper-oxide batteries at each station as a power source, and left the acetylene equipment on the point as a backup in case the batteries failed. The Manitou Island keepers serviced both stations, with assistance coming from the keepers at Eagle Harbor and Mendota light-stations if necessary.7

Leasing of the lighthouse

During the 1920s, in an effort to cut costs and repairs, the Bureau of Lighthouses began to sell unused portions of lighthouse reservations. Unused portions generally consisted of buildings, privys, storehouses, and land not essential to the lighting apparatus or navigational aid. As a rule the government decided to sell the land and buildings, but at Copper Harbor the lighting apparatus remained in the tower. Therefore, they leased all structures except for the tower, and retained access to landing docks to maintain the light. In April 1927 the bureau advertised for potential lessees in area newspapers. Dr. Robert Vaughan, Warden at Cook County Hospital near Chicago, Illinois, submitted the lone bid. On July 20, 1927, he signed a revocable lease granting him occupancy for five years at a rate of $425, or $85 per year. The contract allowed Vaughan, along with Ole Nelson,

From 1927 to 1957 the federal government leased the Copper Harbor light-station, including the outbuildings and dock. Renters paid between $85.00 and $125.00 per year and stayed at the lighthouse during the summer months.

Francis Gerty and members of the Cook County Vacation Club use of the lighthouse property and outbuildings. Members of the Cook County Vacation Club renewed their lease in 1932, 1937 and 1942, at a rate of $500 per five years. The government leased the Copper Harbor range lighthouse as well. When the lights were automated in 1937 Michael Leary of Calumet, Michigan, rented the range lighthouse at a rate of $60 every two years.[8]

Throughout the leasing of the Copper Harbor lighthouse it remained a popular destination for tourists and local residents who enjoyed hunting, hiking, berrying, and picnicking on lighthouse point. Dr. Stanley Martin, a summer resident since 1926, visited the light on many occasions. "We almost always went by boat," he recalled, "there was really no road from U.S. 41 except a wagon road to the Lake Lily area" (east end of Copper Harbor).

Fortunately, the lighthouse remained in good condition. As a boy Martin traveled to the lighthouse with range lightkeeper Charles Davis and remembered the lighthouse "looks just about as it does now. The steel tower was not there so the light was in the tower house [lantern]."9

Mr. Ken Bracco, another longtime summer resident, recalled hunting rabbits on the point with his father in the 1940s. During the summer months they traveled there by boat and landed at the lighthouse dock. In the fall they walked the "old tote road" which began just past the bridge in front of the range lighthouse. Bracco remembered the route as "[full of] pine snags and windfalls," and nearly impassable. Still, the trail continued along the shoreline, occasionally moving inland following the high points of conglomerate, until reaching "Corgan's Cove" along the shore. According to Bracco the name "Corgan's Cove" referred to the location of Henry Corgan's fishing business which consisted of a fish house and dock. From there the trail moved inland, following the conglomerate ridge until it ended "directly behind the lighthouse where the parking lot is now located."10

Dr. Martin also recalled that Charles Davis locked the lighthouse while he served as caretaker, but after he retired in 1930 it remained open to the public. Mr. Bracco confirmed Martin's statement, noting that the lighthouse "was always open, you could go in there anytime." He remembered visiting the point in 1950 (prior to the Vincent lease), and his account sheds light on the lighthouse's interor:

> The inside of the buildings were unlocked. . . . We entered through the back door [and] in the first room there was stove just to the right of the steps. . . . I remember a lot of plaster on the floor and a lot of paper scattered about. . . . In the first room there was an old table and chairs.
>
> On the second floor there was a room that had lots of lighthouse records. There was books of them, and

Many buildings, including the 1848 lightkeeper's dwelling, boathouse and landing, fell into disrepair in the 1950s.

The William Vincent family of Detroit, Michigan, leased the Copper Harbor Lighthouse during the 1950s. They are shown here in the 1866 lighthouse woodshed.

pages torn out of books.... My Dad took them down to the cabin [stone dwelling] to build a fire with them. I remember lots and lots of lighthouse record type material. In the room on the second floor on your right as you're facing east [storeroom]. The inside of the room seemed to be trimmed off in a dirty faded gray.[11]

Following Vaughan's stay at the lighthouse the Coast Guard granted a lease to William Vincent, of Detroit, Michigan, at a rate of $125 per year. The Vincents' rented the dwelling, boathouse, and landing dock from the government for seven years (at two year intervals) until December 31, 1957. According to Mrs. Ruth Vincent, they stayed for four to six weeks at a time and Howard Bergh, a local resident, would bring them across the harbor in his boat. When their lease began, she remembered the buildings were "wide open — and people were very careless about how they used the place." The Vincents' secured the property by installing new locks on the doors and fixing window glass. To deter unwelcome visitors they posted no trespassing signs.

Public access to the lighthouse remained by boat until 1953-54 when the Norland Trust, a group of land owners on the east end of Copper Harbor, subdivided lots and built a road. When William Vincent learned of the project he submitted a proposal to build a road from the lighthouse to the Norland property. The Coast Guard approved, but they would not provide materials or money for the road. Vincent took on the task himself, completing nearly 100 feet of road at his own expense, including a parking area directly behind the lighthouse.[12]

Sale of the Lighthouse

By the 1950s, the lighthouse property fell into disrepair and the buildings were in poor condition. On December 8, 1953, the Coast Guard declared the Copper Harbor lighthouse reservation as "excess" and turned the property over

In 1958 the State of Michigan acquired the lighthouse property as part of Fort Wilkins State Park. Note that the boathouse (far right foreground) is still standing.

to the General Services Administration for sale. A Board of Survey examined the buildings and reported that the lighthouse and privy were in good structural condition except for the deterioration of the brickwork. The 1848 keeper's dwelling, however, had "settlement cracks throughout" and the window frames and sash showed signs of "rot." The boathouse and dock were also in poor condition. The report mentioned that the boathouse doors were missing, and dock's decking had "washed away." In June of 1955 the lighthouse reservation (including Porter's Island) was put up for sale, and on January 28, 1957, the State of Michigan purchased 46.15 acres for $5,000. The Coast

Guard retained 1.1 acres on the tip of the point, including the steel tower, for navigational purposes.[13] The state (Department of Natural Resources, DNR) purchased the land to expand Fort Wilkins State Park and planned to make the lighthouse a maritime museum for park visitors. The DNR made several changes at the lighthouse and restored, replaced, and removed some original fixtures. They buried power lines, removed paint from the 1866 tower by sandblasting, repaired the tower and dwelling roof, replaced brickwork on the chimney, and removed the original sidewalks, steps, and shutters around the 1866 lighthouse. They also replaced floor joists, stabilized interior floors, and extensively replastered and repainted the walls.

In preparation for the nation's Bicentennial celebration the DNR and Michigan History Division (Michigan Historical Center) installed exhibits in the lighthouse. Maritime exhibits were installed by the DNR in the wood shed, kitchen, and parlor, and the History Division installed period furnishings in the first floor bedroom and oil storage room and in the master bedroom on the second floor. The two agencies also installed an interpretive trail consisting of artifacts and portions of shipwrecks raised from the harbor. The trail also included a few signs detailing local geography and early mining efforts on the point. In 1975 the lighthouse was dedicated and opened to visitors. A boat concessionaire was hired by the DNR to bring visitors to the point from the Copper Harbor Marina, and except for a brief period in the 1980s the lighthouse has remained open to the public each year during the summer months.

Interpretation and restoration of the lighthouse continued based on archaeological, architectural and historical research. Throughout the 1990s the DNR and Michigan Historical Center worked closely to improve, interpret and preserve the lighthouse museum. In 1994, based on architectural and historical research, workers put a new metal shingled roof on the 1866

In 1998, in observance of the 150th anniversary of the Copper Harbor light, the Michigan Historical Center installed new exhibits in the 1848 keeper's house.

Based on historical and archaeological clues, exhibits in the 1866 lighthouse depict a c.1910 lighthouse as a workplace and home. The parlor's Victrola is shown here.

lighthouse (and the Copper Harbor range lighthouse). For five weeks during the summer of 1994 Michigan Technological University's Industrial History and Archaeology Program conducted archaeology on the site of the first Copper Harbor light tower. In 1996, further restoration and interpretation included installation of period exhibits in the 1866 lighthouse, and after twenty-five years the Center installed new exhibits (with period furnishings) in the downstairs kitchen, woodshed, parlor, office and oil room. These exhibits, based on collected data from other Lake Superior lighthouses, interpret life at a lighthouse and let visitors view what a lighthouse may have looked like during the early 1900s.

In 1997, as part of the four-year restoration effort (through a federal Coastal Land Management Grant and matching funds), the DNR repaired and replaced the roof, windows, doors and floors in the 1848 keeper's dwelling. In addition, a paint analysis was conducted to determine the original color of the interior and exterior of the 1848 dwelling and 1866 lighthouse. Workers painted both buildings to match the historical record as closely as possible. To celebrate the light's 150th anniversary, the lighthouse complex was rededicated on August 6, 1998, when the Michigan Historical Center completed installation of new exhibits. The "new" Copper Harbor Lighthouse Museum now consists of the 1848 keeper's dwelling, 1866 lighthouse, 1933 steel tower and outdoor interpretive paths. "Hands-on" activities and computer interactive programs highlight the exhibit.

Today, the Copper Harbor lighthouse stands as a silent reminder of a time when keepers served an important role in Lake Superior shipping. Although it no longer has a resident keeper, thousands of people visit the site during the summer months. Through the State of Michigan's efforts, visitors to Fort Wilkins State Park have the opportunity to learn about an important piece of maritime history, and the story of a remote lighthouse on Michigan's Keweenaw Peninsula.

APPENDIX
CONTRACT FOR BUILDING THE COPPER HARBOR LIGHTHOUSE

August 21, 1847
(National Archives RG 26, Deeds and Contracts)

"This agreement made the twenty first day of August in the year one thousand eight hundred and forty seven between Charles Rude of Sandusky City in the State of Ohio of the first part and Samuel K. Haring, Collector of the District of Michilimackinac in the State of Michigan of the second part Witnesseth, ...

That said party of the first part for and in consideration of four thousand and eight hundred dollars to be paid to him by the said party of the second part upon the completion and approval by the party of the second part. . . . It shall be built upon such spot as the party of the second part shall designate at Copper Harbor in Lake Superior in the State of Michigan of the following materials, dimensions and descriptions.

The lighthouse to be built of split stone or hard bricks in the form round. The foundation to be sunk three feet, or deeper as may be necessary to make the fabric secure, to be built up solid, and laid in good lime mortar. The tower to be sixty five feet high from the surface of the ground, the diameter of the base to be twenty five feet and that of the top twelve feet, the thickness of the walls at the base to be five feet and to be uniformly graduated to two feet at the top. The top to be arched on which is to be laid a deck of soap stone or other stone of a proper quality fourteen and a half feet in diameter and five inches thick and joints filled in with white lead. On one side of the deck a scuttle door twenty four inches by twenty inches the scuttle door an iron frame covered with copper, the outside wall is to be pointed with Romany cement and whitewashed twice over, there are to be six windows in the tower, of twelve lights each of ten by eight glass in strong frames and a door of five feet by three feet made of double inch boards cross nailed with substantial hinges, with lock and latch the ground floor to be paved with brick or stone.

A sufficient number of circular steps leading from the ground floor to within six feet of the lantern connected by a center post, the stairs to be made of yellow Pine clear of sap and well seasoned, the stairs and floor to be two inch planks (planed). From the top of the stairs to the entrance of the scuttle door to be an iron ladder with steps two and a half inches square.

On the top of the tower to be an iron lantern of an octagon form the posts to be two inches square, to run down five feet into the stone or brick work and secured with anchor. The height and diameter of the lantern to sufficient to admit an iron sash in each octagon to contain fifteen lights fifteen by twenty four glass with a tier of copper panes at bottom the rabbets of the sashes to be three quarters of an inch deep and glazed with an iron framed door covered with copper four feet by two in the clear, to be shut tight with the rabbets with a strong turned button. The top to be a dome framed by sixteen iron rafters concentrating in an iron hoop five inches wide nine inches diameter, covered with copper thirty two ounces to the square foot which is to come down and rivet in the piece that forms the top of the sash, which is to be three inches wide. On the dome to be a traversing ventilator two and a half feet long and fifteen inches diameter, to which is to be secured a copper vane three feet long and twenty inches wide. The ventilator and vane to be framed with iron, covered with copper and painted black.

Around the lantern to be an iron railing, the posts of which to be one and three eights of an inch square connected by three railings three quarter of an inch square, the upper one to be four feet from the decks. The lantern and wood work of the tower to be painted twice over with white lead except the dome which is to be black lantern inside.

The lighthouse to have a complete electrical conductor, made of copper three quarters of an inch in diameter with an improved electrical point to be substantially secured with proper bolts and stays to base tower and dome to extend in height at least four feet above the top of the ventilator or vane, and in depth at least four feet into the earth forming an obtuse angle from the perpendicular of the foundation of the lighthouse.

The dwelling house to be of split stone or hard brick thirty four feet by twenty from out to out one story of eight feet in the clear, divided into two rooms with an entry between, the stairs to lead to the chambers and the cellar to be in entry. A chimney with a fire place in each room with iron or stove bricks on sides, a cellar under the whole of the house, with sufficient walls of stone to support the walls of the house which are to be twenty inches thick, the whole laid up in strong fine mortar and to be well pointed. The roof to be rectangular, the boards of which to be jointed and halved, the roof joists to be not less than eight inches by three at the ridge and three inches by seven at the foot with collar beams seven inches by three, the joists to be placed not over two feet apart to be well secured and covered with first quality shingles. There are to be three windows in each room, of sixteen lights of eight by ten glass each, and one of the same dimensions in each chamber. The doors to be four paneled with first quality hinges and thumb latch to each a good lock on the outside door with a bolt and thumb latch to back passage door. A closet in each room with a good lock to it, all the floors to be doubled and well nailed, the joists of the first floor to be twelve by three inches, and of the second to be ten by three inches square, to be laid not exceeding two feet apart.

Also a kitchen attached to the dwelling house, fourteen feet by twelve in the clear, the walls of the stone or brick eight feet high with double floors the joists of the first floor to be twelve by two inches and of the second ten by three inches square, two windows and one door besides a door to communicate with the dwelling house a chimney with a fire place and sizable oven with an iron door, iron brace, trammel and hooks in the fire place and on one side of the chimney a sink with a spout leading through the wall.

Also an out house or privy at a convenient distance from the dwelling of stone or brick five feet by four in the clear, with a well at least eight feet deep, walled with stone or brick, the roof to be well shingled.

Also a well to be sunk of such a depth as to procure good water, at a distance from the house to be stoned or bricked up and furnished with a pump, or with a curl, windlass and an iron chain; and a strong iron hooped bucket.

All the wood work of the dwelling house, kitchen and outhouse to be painted with two coats of good paint exclusive of priming. The inside walls and ceilings to be lathed and plastered and finished in a plain neat style gutters of double tin to lead round the dwelling house and kitchen, with spouts of same material to carry off the rain water. All the lumber used to be of well seasoned heart pine, consequently entirely free from sap.

Above and below each window frame of the lighthouse must be single stone of sufficient dimensions to reach from out to out of the frame and extend inward the whole thickness of the wall. And in building up the walls, if of stone there must be an entire range of thorough stones every three feet beside that in the intermediate space the stone must tie.

The lighthouse is also to be fitted up in the same manner that the lighthouses of the United States have been fitted up by Winslow Lewis with thirteen patent lamps, and thirteen fourteen inch reflectors — reflectors to be made in dies or moulds [sic] as done by Winslow Lewis and by Hooper and Co. of Boston Massachusetts, each reflector to have six ounces of pure silver and to furnish two spare lamps and reflectors double tin oil butts to hold five hundred gallons of oil one lantern canister and an iron trivet, one stove and one funnel, one two wick box, one tin tube box, one oil carrier, one oil feeder, six wick formers, one hand lantern and lamp, two tube cleaners, one glaziers diamond, two files, and two pair of scissors.

The whole to be completed in a workman like manner by the first day of July next, subject to the approval of the Collector of Michilimackinac or of such persons as he shall appoint for that purpose.

And said party of the second part as Collector as a foresaid does covenant and agree for himself and his successors in office to pay to said party of the first part upon the completion approval and delivery of all the work specified the sum of Four thousand eight hundred Dollars."

BIBLIOGRAPHY

Articles, Books, Government Documents and Unpublished Works

Adams, W.H.
1871 *Light Houses and Light Ships: A descriptive and historical account of their mode of construction and organization.* London, New York: T. Nelson and Sons.

Adamson, Hans Christian
1955 *Keepers of the Lights.* New York: Greenburg.

Anonymous
1856 "Lighthouse construction and Illumination," *General Technology,* Vol. 4. Library of Congress.

Bancroft, William L.
1892 "Memoir Of Capt. Samuel Ward With A Sketch Of The Early Commerce Of The Upper Great Lakes," *Historical Collections,* Michigan Pioneer and Historical Society. (21):358-361.

Bertrand, Lewis B. and Oliver T. Burnham
1971 "Lake Carrier's Association," *Inland Seas.* Cleveland: Great Lakes Historical Society. Vol. 27 (3):163-167.

Carter, James L. and Ernest H. Rankin, eds.
1970 *North to Lake Superior. The Journal of Charles W. Penny 1840.* Marquette, Michigan: John M. Longyear Research Library.

Chance, James T.
1867 *On Optical Apparatus Used In Lighthouses.* Excerpt Minutes of Proceedings of The Institution of Civil Engineers. XXVI, Session 1866-67.

Chaput, Donald
1971 *The Cliff: America's First Great Copper Mine.* Kalamazoo, Michigan: Sequoia Press.

Chase, Mary Ellen
1965 *The Story of Lighthouses.* New York: Norton.

Childs, W.A.
> 1905 "Reminiscences of Old Keweenaw," *Historical Collections*, Michigan Pioneer and Historical Society. (30):150-55.

Claudy, C.H.
> 1907 "Lighthouse Service of the United States," *World Today*, Vol. 12:124-126.

Conklin, Irving
> 1939 *Guideposts to the Sea.* New York: Macmillan Co.

Evans, Captain Steven H. USCG
> 1949 *The U.S. Coast Guard 1790-1915.* Annapolis: U.S. Naval Academy.

Fadner, Lawrence T. ed.
> 1976 *Fort Wilkins 1844 and the U.S. Mineral Land Agency 1843.* New York: Vantage Press.

Fisher, James
> 1945 "Fort Wilkins," *Michigan History Magazine*, (30):158.

Frazer, John F. Ed.
> 1852 "Extract from the Report of the Secretary of the Treasury on Light-Houses of the United States," *Journal of the Franklin Institute.* Third Series, Volume XXIII. Philadelphia: Franklin Institute. 232-239.

Friggens, Thomas
> 1985 "Fort Wilkins Living History Manual," unpublished manuscript on file at Fort Wilkins State Park, Copper Harbor, Michigan.

Gray, Hanna Brockway
> 1936 "Letters from Long Ago," *Michigan History Magazine*, (20):190-191.

Havinghurst, Walter
> 1961 *The Long Ships Passing: The Story of the Great Lakes.* New York: The Macmillan Co.

Hague, Douglas B.
> 1975 *Lighthouses: their architecture, history, and archaeology.* London: Gomer Press.

Heap, D.P.
> 1889 *Ancient and Modern Lighthouses.* Boston: Tinknor and Company.

Holland, Francis Ross Jr.
> 1972 *America's Lighthouses; An Illustrated History.* New York: Dover Publications Inc. 1-54.

1968 *The Old Point Loma Lighthouse: Symbol of the Pacific Coast's First Lighthouses.* San Diego: Cabrillo Historical Assoc. reprinted 1978.

Hyde, Charles K.
1987 *The Northern Lights.* Detroit: Wayne State University Press.

James, Barry C., and Grant Day
1995 *History and Archaeology of the First Copper Harbor Lighthouse: Report of Investigations Number 21.* Houghton: Michigan Technological University Department of Social Sciences Archaeology Laboratory.

Johnson, Arthur Burges
1889 *The Modern Lighthouse Service.* Washington, D.C.

Kaler, J.O.
1906 *Lightkeepers of the U.S. Lighthouse Service.* New York: E.P. Dutton and Co.

Kobbe, G.
1894 "Life in a Lighthouse," *The Century Illustrated Monthly Magazine.* (47) New Series (25):364-374.

Kozma, LuAnne G., Ed.
1987 *Living at a Lighthouse: Oral Histories from the Great Lakes.* Allen Park, Michigan: Great Lakes Lighthouse Keepers Association.

Krause, David
1992 *The Making of a Mining District.* Detroit: Wayne State University Press.

Lankton, Larry
1997 *Beyond the Boundaries:Life and Landscape at the Lake Superior Copper Mines, 1840 - 1875.* Oxford: Oxford University Press.

Lawrence, Charles B.
1954 "Keweena Portage," *Michigan History,* (38):45-64.

Lewis Publishing Company
1895 *Memorial Record of the Northern Peninsula of Michigan.* Chicago.

Mason, Philip P. (ed.)
1958 *Schoolcraft's Expedition to Lake Itasca: The Discovery of the Source of the Mississippi.* East Lansing: The Michigan State University Press.

McCormick, W.H.
1936 *The Modern Book of Lighthouses, Lifeboats and Lightships.* London: Morson & Gibbs.

Munro, Kirk
   1896 "From Light to Light," *Scribner's Monthly Magazine*. Vol. 20.

Noble, Dennis L and T. Michael O'Brien
   1979 *Sentinels of the Rocks: From "Graveyard Coast" to National Lakeshore*. Marquette, Michigan: Northern Michigan University Press.

Nordhoff, Charles
   1874 "The Lighthouses of the United States," *Harper's Weekly Magazine*. Vol. 38 (March).

O'Brien, T. Michael
   1977 *Guardians of the Eighth Sea: A History of the U.S. Coast Guard on the Great Lakes*. Washington, D.C.

Piper, J.
   1925 "Mind the Light Katie! and for 24 Years She Minded It," *American Magazine*. (100):66-67.

Pitezel, John H.
   1859 *Lights and Shades of Missionary Life*. Cincinnati: Western Book Concern.

Putnam, George R.
   1933 *Lighthouses and Lightships of the United States*. Boston: Houghton Mifflin Co.

---

   c.1937 *Sentinel of the Coasts: The Log of a Lighthouse Engineer.* New York: W.W. Norton & Co.

Ritchie, James S.
   1857 *Wisconsin and Its Resources; with Lake Superior, Its Commerce and Navigation*. Philadelphia: Charles Desilver.

Rivot, M.L.E.
   1855 *Voyage Au Lak SupÄriur. Libraires Des Corps ImpÄriaux Des Ponts et ChaussÄes et Des Mines*. Paris: Victor Dalmont E'diteur.

Ryder, Alfred P.
   1861 *Heads Of Enquiry Into The State And Condition Of Lighthouses*. London: Harrison and Sons.

St. John, John R.
   1846 *A True Description of the Lake Superior Country; Its Rivers, Bays, Harbours, Islands, and Commerce*. New York: William H. Graham.

Sawyer, Alvah L.
   1911 *A History of the Upper Peninsula of Michigan and its People*. Chicago: The Lewis Publishing Co.

Scott, George
　1892　*Scott's New Coast Pilot for the Lakes.* Fourth Edition. Detroit: The Free Press Publishing Company.

Sheina, Robert L.
　1987　"Lighthouse, Then and Now." Supplement to *Commandant's Bulletin.* Washington, D.C.: U.S. Coast Guard.

Sterling, Robert Thayer
　1935　*Lighthouses of the Maine Coast and the Men Who Keep Them.* Brattleboro, Vermont: Stephen Daye Press. 43-61.

Stevenson, Thomas
　1859　*Lighthouse Illumination: Being A Description Of The Holophotal System, And Of Azimuthal-Condensing, And Apparent Lights, With Other Improvements.* London: John Weale.

　1881　*Lighthouse Construction and Illumination.* London & New York.

Stobridge, Truman R.
　1974　*Aids to Navigation and the Old Lighthouse Service, 1716-1939.* Washington, D.C.

Struthers and Company
　1855　*Description and Plans of Lights of Lighthouses According To The Catadioptric System Of Augustin Fresnel And The Holophotal System And Other Improvements,* "Collected Papers on Lighthouses." D.H. Hill Library, North Carolina State University.

Thompson, Thomas
　1869　*Thompson's Coast pilot for the Upper Lakes, on both shores, from Chicago to Buffalo, Green Bay, Georgian Bay and Lake Superior.* Detroit: Thomas Thompson. 86.

Updike, Richard W.
　1968　"Winslow Lewis and the Lighthouses," *The American Neptune* 28 (January) Number 1.

U.S. Bureau of Lighthouses
　1925　*Lighthouse Service Bulletin,* Volume 3:(21). Washington, D.C.

U.S. Lighthouse Board
　1870　*Instructions and Directions to Guide-Lighthouse Keepers and Other Belonging to the Light-House Establishment.* Washington, D.C.

U.S. Lighthouse Board
　1881　*Instructions and Directions to Light-house and Light Vessel Keepers of the United States.* Washington, D.C.: GPO.

U.S. Lighthouse Board
> 1902 *Instructions and Directions to Light-house and Light Vessel Keepers of the United States.* Washington, D.C.

U.S. Lighthouse Establishment
> 1937 *Book of References and Standards.* Washington, D.C.

Weiss, George
> 1926 *The Lighthouse Service, Its History, Activities, and Organization.* Baltimore: The John Hopkins Press.

Western Historical Company
> 1883 *History of the Upper Peninsula of Michigan.* Chicago. 328-337.

Whitney, J.D.
> 1854 *The Metallic Wealth Of The United States.* Philadelphia: Lippincott, Grambo & Co.

Wolffe, Julian F.
> 1990 *Lake Superior Shipwrecks.* Duluth, Minnesota: Lake Superior Port Cities.

Archival Documents

Michigan Technological University Archives and Copper Country Historical Collections. Houghton, Michigan.
> Microfilm, Accession #318, Copper Harbor Range Light Station: Selected Documents from the National Archives including appointment of keepers, Lighthouse Board, and Inspections in the 11th District. c. 1851-early 1900.
>
> "Records of the board of school inspectors and of the district board school district No. 1, 1856-1881."

The National Archives, Washington, D.C.
> Record Group 26, Records of the United States Coast Guard, Lighthouse Service.

Interviews and Personal Communication

Ken Bracco, Oral Interview, 1995.

Stanley Martin, Personal Communication, 1995.

Ruth Vincent, Oral Interview, 1996.

Newspapers

The Daily Mining Gazette. Houghton, Michigan.

The Daily Mining Journal. Marquette, Michigan.

The Detroit Daily Free Press. Detroit, Michigan.

The Milwaukee Sentinel. Milwaukee, Wisconsin.

ENDNOTES

Chapter 1
The Lighthouse Service and Copper Harbor, 1840-1846

1. George Putnam, *Lighthouses And Lightships Of The United States* (Boston, 1933), 31-35.
2. Arnold B. Johnson, *The Modern Lighthouse Service* (Washington, D.C., 1890), 17-19.
3. Francis R. Holland Jr., *America's Lighthouses; Their Illustrated History Since 1716* (Brattleboro, Vermont, 1972), 30-36.
4. *Annual Report of the Lighthouse Board*, (Washington, D.C., 1868, 1876). Hereafter, AR LHB; and Charles K. Hyde, *The Northern Lights: Lighthouses of The Upper Great Lakes* (Detroit, 1986), 20.
5. James L. Carter and Ernest H. Rankin, eds., *North to Lake Superior. The Journal of Charles W. Penny 1840* (Marquette, 1970); and David Krause, *The Making of A Mining District* (Detroit, 1992), 25.
6. Carter and Rankin, 47-49.
7. *History of the Upper Peninsula of Michigan* (Chicago, 1883), 336.
8. Lawrence T. Fadner, *Fort Wilkins 1844 and the U.S. Mineral Land Agency 1843* (New York, 1966), 153-58.
9. James Fisher, "Fort Wilkins," *Michigan History Magazine*, XXX:158; Donald Chaput, *The Cliff: America's First Great Copper Mine* (Kalamazoo, 1971), 19-20.
10. Fadner, 23-28.
11. James S. Ritchie, *Wisconsin and Its Resources; with Lake Superior, Its Commerce and Navigation* (Philadelphia, 1857), 194.
12. *Report Of The President and Directors Of The Pittsburgh and Boston Mining Company* (Pittsburgh, 1849), 5-7. Hereafter, *PB Annual Report*, 1849.
13. For a description of the topography and early mining locations at Copper Harbor see William Ives' "Subdivision of T52N R28W of the first Meridian Mich. Begun August 29, 1845, Finished September 3, 1845," State Archives of Michigan RG 87-155. DNR Survey Notes, Box 48, Vol. 1747.
14. John R. St. John, *A True Description of the Lake Superior Country; Its Rivers, Bays, Harbours, Islands, and Commerce* (New York, 1846), 80-81; and *PB Annual Report* 1849, 6.
15. J.D. Whitney, *The Metallic Wealth Of The United States* (Philadelphia, 1854), 275.
16. *PB Annual Report*, 1849, 7.
17. Horace V. Winchell, *Historical Sketch of the Mineral Deposits of the Lake Superior Region* (Lansing, 1894), 13.

18. 28th Congress of the United States, 2nd Session, "Report of the Secretary of War 1845," Senate Document 117:3.
19. John Cummings, *The John Jacob Astor* (Mount Pleasant, Michigan, 1981).
20. *Lake Superior News,* 5 September 1846. Hereafter, LSN.
21. Charles B. Lawrence, "Keweena Portage," *Michigan History,* (38):45-64.
22. Philip P. Mason (ed.), *Schoolcraft's Expedition to Lake Itasca: The Discovery of the Source of the Mississippi* (Lansing, 1958), 175-76.
23. Rev. John H. Pitezel, *Lights and Shades of Missionary Life,* (Cincinnati, 1882), 236.
24. 28th Congress of the United States, 2nd Session, "Report of the Secretary of War 1845," Senate Document 117:3.
25. St. John, 110.
26. *LSN,* 29 August 1846.
27. William L. Bancroft, "Memoir Of Capt. Samuel Ward With A Sketch Of The Early Commerce Of The Upper Great Lakes," *Historical Collections, Michigan Pioneer and Historical Society,* XXI:358-361.

Chapter 2
The Copper Harbor Light

1. *Laws of Michigan,* Senate Document 78:104.
2. 30th Congress of the United States, 2nd Session, Senate Document 27:15.
3. Record Group 26, Records of the United States Coast Guard, Lighthouse Service, Index of Correspondence, Letters Received by the Lighthouse Board 1852-1900, Letter Book 83:1. Hereafter, NARG 26 Index of Correspondence with reference. By Executive Order of December 9, 1852, Congress implied that the lighthouse reservation was temporary. Therefore, by the same order the following land was reserved for lighthouse purposes; Fractional Sections 27 and 28 on the mainland; Lot 1, Section 33 on the east cape of the Harbor; and Lot 2, Section 29, and Lots 3 and 4, Section 32, on Porters Island, all in Township 59 N., Range 28 W., comprising a total area of 47.25 acres.
4. NARG 26, *Annual Reports,* 1852. Hereafter, *Annual Report* with date.
5. *Lake Superior News and Miners Journal* 12 June 1847. Hereafter, LSNMJ.
6. Anonymous, "Lighthouse Construction and Illumination," *General Technology,* Vol. 4, August 1856, 198.
7. NARG 26, *Correspondence Relating to Early Lighthouses, Letters Received from the Superintendent of Lights 1803-1852,* Box 3. Letter, Stephen Pleasonton to Samuel Haring 18 August 1847. Hereafter, *Early Lighthouses* with reference.
8. NARG 26, *Deeds and Contracts,* Vol. H:105-110., Hereafter, *Deeds and Contracts,* Vol. H:105-110. Rude submitted the lowest bid for building the tower, dwelling, and installing the lighting apparatus in the lantern.
9. NARG 26, *Letters Received from the Superintendent of Lights 1803-1852,* Box 3. Letter from Samuel K. Haring to Pleasonton, May 20, 1848.
10. NARG 26, *Early Lighthouses, Draft Copies of Letters Sent,* Sept. 1847-May 1848, Box 18. Letters from Robert J. Walker to Haring, 6 August and 18 August 1848. Hereafter, *Draft Copies* with reference.

11. *Deeds and Contracts, Vol. H*:105-110.
12. NARG 26, "Light-House Letters," Series P, 1844-1864 Box 5, 1844-1848. Letter from John W. Allen to the Secretary of the Treasury, 28 May 1850.
13. In 1994 the author examined the lighthouse property and noted that the Pittsburgh and Boston works consisted of a few pits and exploratory trenches. Very little waste rock remained near these features.
14. *Report to the Lighthouse Board,* 3 July 1851.
15. *Deeds and Contracts, Vol. H*:105-110.
16. Barry James and Grant Day, *History and Archaeology of the First Copper Harbor Lighthouse.* (Houghton: Michigan Technological University 1995); and Douglas B. Hague, *Lighthouses: their architecture, history, and archaeology* (London 1975), 101.
17. Ibid.
18. Holland, 14-16.
19. Ibid.
20. For a detailed summary of lighthouse illumination see Thomas Stevenson, *Lighthouse Construction and Illumination* (London & New York 1881), 56-59.
21. M.L.E. Rivot, *Voyage Au Lak SupÄriur. Libraires Des Corps ImpÄriaux Des Ponts et ChaussÄes et Des Mines* (Paris, 1855), 22.
22. *Annual Report of the Lighthouse Board,* 1867. Hereafter, *AR LHB* with reference.
23. Anonymous, 208.
24. *Journal of the Copper Harbor Range Light Station,* 20 September 1879. Copies on file at Fort Wilkins State Park, Copper Harbor, MI. Hereafter, *RLJ* with reference; *AR LHB*, 1886.
25. NARG 26, Letters Sent Regarding the Lighthouse Service, 1792-1852, Vol 30. Letter from George Withrell to Charles Avery 7 June 1849. Hereafter, *Letters Sent* with reference.
26. NARG 26, Descriptive Lists of Lighthouse Stations 1858:18-24., Hereafter, *Descriptive List 1858.*
27. Ibid.
28. James and Day, 55-67.
29. *Early Lighthouses, Letters Received,* Box 20, Letter from Charles Rude to Stephen Pleasonton, 15 January 1850.
30. NARG 26, *Official Register of Lighthouse Keepers, 1845-1900.* Hereafter, ORLHK.
31. *Early Lighthouses, Letters Received,* Box 20, Letter from Charles E. Avery to S. Pleasonton, 5 June 1849.
32. *Lake Superior Journal,* 5 June 1850. Hereafter, LSJ.
33. *Early Lighthouses, Letters Received,* Box 20. Letter from Charles Avery to Pleasonton, 6 March 1850; and NARG 26, Annual Reports 1820-1853, Box 3., "Report in regard to the Light Houses in the District of Michilimackinac, 1851," Letter from Charles E. Avery, Sup't of Lights Michilimackinac, to Thorton A. Jenkins, Lt. U.S.N, Secretary of the Lighthouse Board.

34. NARG 26, Annual Reports 1820-1853, Box 3., "Report in regard to the Light Houses in the District of Michilimackinac, 1851," Letter from Charles E. Avery, Sup't of Lights Michilimackinac, to Thorton A. Jenkins, Lt. U.S.N, Secretary of the Lighthouse Board.
35. ORLHK.
36. *Laws and Regulations,* (Washington, D.C., 1881), 54-55.
37. *Descriptive List 1858*:18-24, and AR LHB, 1856, and George Putnam, *Lighthouses And Lightships Of The United States* (Boston, 1933), 128.
38. Struthers and Company, *Description and Plans of Lights of Lighthouses* (Birmingham, 1855), 1-19.
39. *Lake Superior Miner,* 1 December 1855. Hereafter, LSM.
40. Letter John Beedon to J. Wendell, 28 December 1855. Central Michigan University, Clark Historical Library: Wendell Papers Light House Service, Mount Pleasant, Michigan. Copy on file at Fort Wilkins State Park, Beedon File.
41. *LSM,* 8 March 1856.
42. Index of Correspondence, Letter Book 46:230, 26 May 1857; Letter Book 94:221, 31 May, 1857; and NARG 26, *Letter's Sent to District Inspectors and Engineers,* Oct. 1852-July 1939, Letter Book 89:303, Letter from Naval Comdr. R. Semmer (?) USN, to 11th District Inspector, 3 June 1859.
43. *Milwaukee Sentinel* 18 November 1857, and LSM 28 November 1857.
44. *Detroit Daily Free Press* 17 November 1857; *Ontonagon Miner* 5 December and 16 December 1857.
45. NARG 26, Letters Received from District Engineers and Inspectors, Feb. 1853-Dec. 1900. Box 314, Letter Book 162, Part II. Letter from Engineer's office, 10th & 11th LH Districts, Detroit Joshua Barney, US Lake Survey, 10 August 1863. Hereafter, *Letters Rec'd District Inspectors* with reference.
46. Ibid.
47. Captain Robert Harris, Personal Communication, 1994.
48. *Letters Rec'd District Inspectors,* Letter Book 162, Part II, Box 314.
49. See *Plan for constructing lighthouses at Turtle Is., Lake Erie, Marquette, Copper Harbor & Ontonagon, Lake Superior;* and Index of Correspondence, Letter Book 175:17; State Archives of Michigan, RG 80-32, Drawer 12, File 13.
50. *AR LHB*, 1865; For the map see *Proposed Plan for rebuilding Light Houses at Marquette and Copper Harbor 1866,* copy on file at the Marquette County Historical Society, Marquette, Michigan, Drawer 18. Original on file at the United States Coast Guard Academy, New London, Connecticut.
51. Index of Correspondence, Letter Book 165:208; and *AR LHB*, 1860.
52. *Letters Rec'd Inspectors,* Letter Book 234:51; Index of Correspondence 17 Sept. 1868; and *AR LHB,* 1868.
53. *LSJ,* 21 June 1855, and *AR LHB,* 1894:237.
54. *Lake Superior Mining And Manufacturing News,* 24 October 1867.
55. Limited information on the demise of the first Copper Harbor light tower appears in Hyde, *The Northern Lights,* 76. However, the 1848 Copper Harbor light tower deteriorated because of rain water, not wave action from Lake Superior.

56. James and Day, 192-93.
57. *AR LHB,* 1866.
58. *Letters Rec'd Inspectors,* Letter Book 462, Part 1.
59. In 1997 the Michigan Historical Center contracted with Seebohm, LTD., to determine the original paint colors of the 1866 lighthouse and privy, and the 1848 keeper's dwelling. For a more detailed description see *Historic Paint Study: Copper Harbor Lighthouse Complex, Copper Harbor Michigan.* Copy on file at the Michigan Iron Industry Museum, Negaunee, Michigan.
60. *History of the Upper Peninsula of Michigan,* 336.
61. *Letters Rec'd Inspectors,* Letter Book 597:140-42, and 598 Part 1:72-78.
62. Ibid.
63. RLJ, 6 October 1883.
64. Lewis B. Bertrand and Oliver T. Burnham, "Lake Carrier's Association," *Inland Seas* (Cleveland, 1971), Vol. 27 (3):165.
65. *Letters Rec'd Inspectors,* Letter Book 749:420 and 750:522.
66. *The Mining Journal,* 19 May 1888.

Chapter 3
Work and Life at the Copper Harbor Lighthouse

1. Johnson, 102.
2. Putnam, 235.
3. NARG 26, Letters Received From the Superintendent of Lights, 1803-1852, Box 20.
4. George Weiss, *The Lighthouse Service, Its History, Activities, and Organization.* (Baltimore, 1926), 72.
5. *Annual Report to the Lighthouse Board,* 1851.
6. RLJ, 30 August 1893.
7. Hyde, 30.
8. *U.S. Lighthouse Board, Instructions and Directions to Guide-Lighthouse Keepers and Other Belonging to the Light-House Establishment* (Washington, D.C., 1870), 14. Hereafter, *Instructions.*
9. *Instructions,* 1870:143; and 1902:53.
10. Ibid.
11. RLJ, July 27, 1901.
12. Letter from Office of the Superintendent, 11th District, to Commissioner of Lighthouses, 9 November 1923. Official Personnel Folder for Charles Davis, St. Louis; Federal Personnel Records Center. Hereafter, OPF Charles Davis.
13. RLJ, 14 June 1875; and 10 May 1891.
14. RLJ, 13 June 1893.
15. NARG 26, Correspondence of the Bureau of Lighthouses, 1911-1939. File 1454E. Letter from Assistant Commissioner to Mr. J.A. Doelle, November 7, 1916. Hereafter, Correspondence of the BOLH. Due in part to Doelle's efforts Houghton and Keweenaw Counties purchased the entire fort property in 1921. In 1923 the property became a state park.

16. RLJ, 10 June 1890; OPF Charles Davis.
17. Munro, 460-61; *AR LHB*, 1893; ORLHK.
18. Johnson, 104; total does not include assistant keepers.
19. *AR LHB*, 1894.
20. *United States Lighthouse Service Annual Report*, 1912:7-8.
21. *Journal of the Gull Rock Light-Station Lake Superior, Mich.*, 8 and 9 Sept., 1877. "Light-House Letters," Series P, 1833-1864, Box 8. Letter from J.F. Driggs M.C., to W.P. Fessenden, Secretary of Treasury, 10 September 1864.
22. Kirk Munro, "From Light to Light," *Scribner's Monthly Magazine*, (January 1896), 460; and *AR LHB*, 1893.
23. J.A. Close, Memorandum 1874, 1875 Eleventh L.H. District, July 14, 1874. Marquette Co. Hist. Society, Longyear Research Library, Marquette, Michigan; and Purchases by the Commissioner of Lighthouses in the open market, etc., Fiscal Year Ending 30 June 1911. (Washington, D.C., Government Printing Office, 1911).
24. *Instructions*, 1881, 30.
25. *AR LHB*, 1894, 236; Holland, 50; and Hyde, 65.
26. Letters Rec'd Inspectors, Letter Book 366-A, Box 323. Letter from Stephen Cocking to Commander W.P. McCann, U.S.A., Inspector 11th District, 26 August 1874.
27. "Copper Harbor Light Station, Selected Documents from the National Archives including Appointment of Keepers, Lighthouse Board Inspection 11th District, c. 1850-early 1900s," Microfilm Accession #318. Houghton, Michigan: Michigan Technological University Archives and Copper Country Historical Collections.
28. Election Record, Keweenaw County, State Archives of Michigan RG 77-106, Box 2; Letters Rec'd Inspectors, Letter Book 1046:58; and Index of Correspondence Letter Book 1031:788.
29. RLJ, 1 June 1879.
30. RLJ, 20 July 1900; 29 June and 25 July 1902.
31. Documentation on the Copper Harbor lightkeepers is incomplete. Unless otherwise noted, the data is located in Record Group 26 (Official Register of Lighthouse Keepers) in the National Archives, Washington, D.C.; National Archives Personnel Record Center (Official Personnel Files) at St. Louis, Missouri; and biographical files located at Fort Wilkins State Park. The keeper's name is listed along with the dates he is known to have worked at Copper Harbor.
32. Assessment Roll Township of Copper Harbor County of Houghton 1857; and RG 77-62, Records of the District #1 School Board, 1856-1881. Lansing: State Archives of Michigan.
33. *United States Census of Houghton County*, 27 July 1850; and Clow File, FWSP.
34. Beedon File, FWSP.
35. Ibid.

36. Dennis L. Nobel and T. Michael O'Brien, *Sentinels Of The Rocks* (Marquette, Michigan: 1979), 10.
37. Power File, FWSP; and Thomas Friggens, *Fort Wilkins Living History Manual,* Unpublished manuscript on file at FWSP, 143-50.
38. Ibid.
39. Records of the District #1 School Board, 1856-1881, Lansing: State Archives of Michigan; Power File, FWSP; Alvah L. Sawyer, *A History of the Upper Peninsula of Michigan and its People.* (Chicago, 1911), 687; and *Memorial Record of the Upper Peninsula of Michigan,* 1895:138.
40. Ibid.
41. *Memorial Record of the Upper Peninsula of Michigan,* 1895:447-48.
42. *United States Census for Houghton County,* 1870. Assessment Roll for the Township of Copper Harbor for the year 1872-1880, Lansing: State Archives of Michigan, RG 77-106.
43. *Letter's Rec'd Inspectors,* Letterbook 547:158-60.
44. *Memorial Record of the Upper Peninsula of Michigan,* 1895:447-48.
45. Corgan File, FWSP.
46. *Letters Sent to Inspectors,* Letterbook 766:974-76. Letter from Henry Corgan to the Secretary of the Lighthouse Board, 23 June 1888.
47. RLJ, 20 November and 26 October 1889.
48. *Letters Rec'd Inspectors,* Letterbook 1031:788; and 1046:58.
49. *Daily Expenditure and General Account of Stores Received and Consumed at the Copper Harbor Light-Station, Lake Superior, Mich.* Copy on file at FWSP and Michigan Technological University Archives.
50. Copper Harbor Range Light Station: Selected Documents from the National Archives including appointment of keepers, Lighthouse Board, and Inspections in the 11th District. c. 1851-early 1900. Michigan Technological University Archives and Copper Country Historical Collections, Microfilm: Accession 313.
51. Corgan file, FWSP.

Chapter 4
Epilogue

1. NARG 26, Lighthouse Site Files 1454 A, Letter from the Commissioner of Lighthouses to the Department of Commerce, Bureau of Lighthouses, 23 January 1919, and OPF Charles Davis, Letter from Office of Inspector 11th District to Commissioner of Lighthouses, 2 July 1919. Hereafter, LH Site Files with reference.
2. NARG 26, Lighthouse Service Bulletin, Volume 3:(21), 1 September 1925.
3. LH Site Files 1454 C, Letter from the Office of Superintendent of Lighthouses, 11th District, to Commissioner of Lighthouses, 10 March 1924.
4. Ibid., File 1454 E, Letter from Charles A. Park to H.D. King, Deputy Commissioner, Department of Commerce, 5 May 1933.

5. Ibid., File 1454 A, Letter from F.C. Hangsbury (?), Assistant Superintendent of Lighthouses 11th District to C.A. Park, Acting Commissioner, Department of Commerce, Bureau of Lighthouses, 23 September 1935.
6. Ibid., File 1454 E, Letter from F.P. Dillon, 11th District Superintendent of Lighthouses, to H.D. King, Deputy Commissioner, Department of Commerce, Bureau of Lighthouses, 9 November 1933 and 15 November 1933.
7. Ibid., Letter from Letter from F.P. Dillon, 11th District Superintendent of Lighthouses, to Department of Commerce, Bureau of Lighthouses, 30 March 1937.
8. Civilian/Occupants Leases File, on file at Fort Wilkins State Park.
9. Dr. Stanley Martin, Personal Communication, 1994.
10. Ken Bracco, Oral Interview, 1995. Micro-cassette tape in possession of author.
11. Ibid.
12. Ruth Vincent Interview, Oral Interview, 1996. Cassette tape and transcript on file at the Michigan Iron Industry Museum, Negaunee, Michigan.
13. LH Site Files, Box 32 Copper Harbor Light Station, Proceedings Of A Board of Survey 8 December 1953; Property To Be Declared Excess B/S 09-210830-7-54, 8 April 1955; and memo granting authority of sale by F.B. Thatcher, Commander, Ninth Coast Guard District, Cleveland, Ohio, 2 October 1958.

PICTURE CREDITS

Pg.#	Source
5	Map by Susan E. Cooper Finney (being a modification of a map in the 1877 *Manual for the Use of the Twenty-ninth Legislature of the State of Michigan* located at the State Archives of Michigan)
7	Michigan Technological University Archives and Copper Country Historical Collections
9	Historical painting by Alvah Bradish, Michigan Historical Museum (painting part of the State Capitol of Michigan collection)
11	State Archives of Michigan
15	Illustration by Leland Benson, Michigan Historical Museum
17	*1850 Report on the Geology and Topography of a portion of the Lake Superior Land District in the State of Michigan* by J.W. Foster and J.D. Whitney
21	State Archives of Michigan, Record Group 59-05, Keweenaw County Geological Map, Box 38, 01135
25	Illustration by Rich Geer, Michigan Historical Museum
27	Illustration by Rich Geer, Michigan Historical Museum (left); *Lighthouse Illumination* by Thomas Stevenson (right)
31	Illustration by Rich Geer, Michigan Historical Museum
35	*Lighthouse Illumination* by Thomas Stevenson
37	*Description and Plans of Lights of Lighthouses* by Struthers and Company
41	National Archives, image computer enhanced by Susan E. Cooper Finney
43	National Archives
45	Michigan Historical Museum
47	National Archives, image computer enhanced by Susan E. Cooper Finney
49	National Archives
59	Michigan Historical Museum
61	Michigan Historical Museum
63	State Archives of Michigan
67	Michigan Technological University Archives and Copper Country Historical Collections
69	Michigan Historical Museum

73	*Annual Report of the Lighthouse Board*, 1894
75	Michigan Historical Museum
77	Michigan Historical Museum
79	Michigan Historical Museum
84	State Archives of Michigan
87	State Archives of Michigan
89	State Archives of Michigan
91	Michigan Historical Museum
93	State Archives of Michigan
95	Michigan Historical Museum
front	Susan E. Cooper Finney, Howell, Michigan
back	Jim Godell Photography, Marquette, Michigan

INDEX

Administration of Lighthouses
    Bureau of Lighthouses, 6
    Department of Commerce, 6
    Department of Transportation, 6
    Department of Treasury, 20
    Secretary of Treasury, 4, 5-6, 22, 27, 32, 53, 74
    U. S. Lighthouse Establishment, 4, 6, 20
Abert, John, 13
Allen, Lt. James, 15
Argand lamps, 27, 28, 56
Avery, Charles, 19, 33, 34

Barbiere & Fenestre, 36
Barney, Joshua, 39-40
Beaser, Capt., 38
Beedon, John A., 38, 74
Beedon, Martha Ann, 74
Beedon, Mary, 75
Beedon, Napoleon, 35, 37, 38, 40, 53
    biography of, 74-76
Bennett, Edwin, 78
Bergh, Howard, 92
Bracco, Ken, 90

Calumet, 49, 60, 70, 71, 73, 81, 89
Chambers, Edward, 53, 79, 82
    biography of, 80

Clark mine, 49, 72, 78
Clary, Capt. Robert, 10
Cleveland Vessel Owners Association, 51
Cliff mine, 12
Clow, Henry, 32, 34, 53, 54
  biography of, 74
Cocking, Stephen, 70
Conkling, Charles H., 71
Cook County Vacation Club, 89
copper
  discovery of, 6
  mining of, 3, 8-13, 49, 72
Copper Harbor
  description of, 7-8, 49-50
  mining at, 8-12
Copper Harbor Lighthouse
  archaeology, 26, 31, 45-46, 96
  congressional legislation, 3-6, 19-20, 22, 35, 42-43, 44
  construction, 23-27, 42, 44
  contract, 22, 24, 26, 31, 32, 97-100
  closing of, 49-52
  first lighthouse, 27-34
  leasing of, 88-92
  sale of, 92-96
Corgan, Charles, 52-54, 71, 76, 80
  biography of, 78-79
Corgan, Elizabeth, 76
Corgan, Emmit, 71
Corgan, Henry, 52-54, 60, 71-73, 85, 90
  biography of, 80-83
Corgan, James, 54, 66, 81
Corgan, Mary Mooney, 78, 80
Cunningham, General Walter, 10

Davis, Charles T., 52, 54, 56, 60-64, 70-71, 73, 82, 83, 85, 90
Delaware mine, 49, 70
Dillon, F. P., 88

fog horns, 55, 66, 68
Fort Brady, 10
Fort Wayne, 76
Fort Wilkins, 10-12, 14, 20, 32, 44, 61-62, 72, 74, 76, 77, 79, 80, 82, 94, 96
Fresnel lens, 6, 19, 55
    description of, 4, 35-36
fuel, for lights, 29, 57, 62, 67, 85-86, 88

Graham, Colonel, 42
Gray, Andrew, 17
"Green Rock" (*La Roche Verte*), 7, 8
Guilbault, Norman, 81
Gull Rock, 15. *See also* lighthouses
Guthrie, James, 74

Hammond, Charles G., 20-22
Hancock, 49, 50
Haring, Samuel K., 22, 97
Harvey, Charles T., 14
Haven, Charles, 88
Hays Point, 11, 12, 16
Hays, John, 11
Henry, Prof. Joseph, 29
Houghton, 49, 50, 68, 71
Houghton, Douglass, 8-9, 15
Hubbard, Bela, 8

Iron City mine, 75
Ives, William, 12

Keweenaw Bay, 15, 74

Keweenaw Peninsula, 3, 7, 10, 24, 28, 29, 53, 55, 68, 72, 74, 78, 80, 96
    description of, 13-14, 16
    native copper at, 7-8, 12, 49
    climate, 59-61

Keweenaw Point, 11, 15, 17, 21, 22, 33, 50, 51, 72, 86

L'Anse, 10, 74

La Point, Wisconsin, 17. *See also* lighthouses

lake boats
    Algonquin (schooner), 14
    Cigar (ore carrier), 60
    City of Superior (steamer), 38-39
    Fanny and Floy (shipping vessel), 44
    Ford (schooner), 37
    Freeman (schooner), 37
    Independence (steamer), 33
    John Jacob Astor (brigantine), 14
    Mather (steamer), 60
    Ogontz (steamer), 36, 37
    Seaman (schooner), 37, 38
    Superior (steamer), 36, 37

Lake Fanny Hooe, 10

Lake Itasca, 16

Lake Superior. *See* shipping and lake boats

Leary, Michael, 89

Lewis, Winslow, 27-28, 35, 100

Lighthouse Board, 19, 26, 29, 36, 38, 40, 42-44, 50-52, 53-54, 60, 62, 64, 70-71, 78, 81, 82
    origins, 6, 35
    publications of, 56

Lighthouse Service, 52, 54, 55, 66, 71, 73, 75, 79, 80, 81, 83, 85
    flag, 65
    inspections, 62

    libraries, 69-70

    origins, 3-6

    provisions for lightkeepers, 58, 68

lighthouse tenders

    Amaranth, 51, 67, 68

    Marigold, 67, 68

    Warrington, 67

    Lotus, 67

lighthouses

    Big Sable (Au Sable), 75

    Bois Blanc, 20

    Eagle Bluff, Wisconsin, 42

    Eagle Harbor, 13, 28, 33, 50, 51, 70, 86, 88

    Escanaba (Sand Point or Peninsula Point), 45, 52, 81

    Grand Island, 42, 44, 75

    Green Island, Wisconsin, 42

    Gull Rock, 29, 50, 51, 54, 56, 64, 65-66, 68, 70, 72, 80, 81

    La Point, Wisconsin, 17

    Manitou Island, 15, 22, 23, 24, 28, 33, 50, 54-55, 64, 65, 66, 68, 76, 78, 81, 86, 88

    Marquette, 34, 42

    Point Iroquois, 80

    Porter's Island, 10, 11, 16, 93

    Pottowatomie, 20

    Presque Isle, 20

    Round Island, 80

    Saginaw Bay, 20, 42

    South Manitou, 20

    St. Mary's River Range Light, 80

    Stannard Rock, 80

    Thunder Bay, 20

    Whitefish Point, 17, 19, 20, 22, 32-33, 34, 75, 79, 80

    Windmill Point, 80

lightkeepers, 4, 23, 32, 34, 37, 38, 42, 49, 50, 52
    appointment of, 53-54, 64
    duties of, 55-61
    entertainment, 72-73
    pay, 54-55
    rations and supplies, 61, 67-69
    uniforms, 64-65

Manitou Island, 15. *See also* lighthouses
Marquette, 8. *See also* lighthouses
Martin, Dr. Stanley, 89-90
Michigan Technological University, 26, 31-32, 45-46, 96
Michilimackinac, 19, 20, 21, 22, 24, 33, 38, 97, 100
Mineral Land Agency, 10, 13
minerals. *See* copper
mining. *See* copper and individual names of mines
Montreal River, 10, 13
Munising, Michigan, 44, 75

navigation. *See* shipping
Native Americans, 7, 8, 10
New York, 67, 76
Nolan, John, 56, 66, 81

oil. *See* fuel
Ontonagon, 10, 33, 37, 38, 39

Park, Charles, 86
Penny, Charles, 3, 8
Phoenix mine, 49
Pitezel, Reverend John H., 16, 33
Pittsburgh and Boston Mining Company, 11-12, 24-25
Pleasonton, Stephen, 4-5, 20, 22, 26, 27, 32, 33
Portage Lake, 44, 49, 50, 70

Power, John, 53, 70-71, 80
    biography of, 76-78
Putnam, George, 6

range lights, 43, 44, 50, 51, 55, 87, 88
Raynolds, Colonel William F., 42, 44
Red Jacket. *See* Calumet
Rich, James W., 51, 53, 82
    biography of, 80
Roosevelt, Franklin D., 6
Rude, Charles, 22-23, 24, 30-32, 97

Sault Ste. Marie, 10, 14
Saunders, George N., 16
Schoolcraft, Henry Rowe, 8, 16
Scott, Frank, 70
Scott, George, 38
shipping and navigation, 3-4, 22, 32, 33, 36-37, 44, 48, 51, 66, 81, 85
    demand for, 13
    difficulties of, 13-18
ships. *See* lake boats
shipwrecks, 60
    City of Superior, 38-39
    John Jacob Astor, 14
Shurter, Henry C., 34-35, 53
    biography of, 74
Smith, Angus McLoud, 55
Smith, William, 82-83
Spaulding, Captain John, 39
St. John, John R., 17
Stannard, Captain Benjamin, 14
Star mine, 49

Toltec Copper Mining Company, 39

Treaty of LaPoint, 8, 10
Tresise, William, 72

uniforms. *See* lightkeepers
United States Coast Guard, 6, 88, 92, 93
United States Lake Survey, 39, 42

Vaughan, Dr. Robert, 88-89, 92
vessels. *See* lake boats
Vincent, Ruth, 91, 92
Vincent, William, 91, 92
voyageurs, 7

Walker, Robert J., 22
Warner, Ebenezar, 32
Watson, James W., 52
Wilkins, William, 11